Beyond Standardized Testing

Better Information for School Accountability and Management

George W. Elford

A SCARECROWEDUCATION BOOK

The Scarecrow Press, Inc.
Lanham, Maryland, and Oxford
2002

A SCARECROWEDUCATION BOOK

Published in the United States of America
by Scarecrow Press, Inc.
A Member of the Rowman & Littlefield Publishing Group
4720 Boston Way, Lanham, Maryland 20706
www.scarecroweducation.com

PO Box 317
Oxford
OX2 9RU, UK

Copyright © 2002 by George W. Elford

All rights reserved. No part of this publication may be reproduced, stored in a retrieval system, or transmitted in any form or by any means, electronic, mechanical, photocopying, recording, or otherwise, without the prior permission of the publisher.

British Library Cataloguing in Publication Information Available

Library of Congress Cataloging-in-Publication Data

Elford, George W.
  Beyond standardized testing : better information for school accountability and management / George W. Elford.
    p. cm.
  Includes index.
  ISBN 0-8108-4386-2 (Cloth : alk. paper)—ISBN 0-8108-4385-4 (paperback : alk. paper)
  1. Educational tests and measurements—Standards—United States. 2. Educational accountability—United States. I. Title.

LB3051 .E456 2002
371.26′2—dc21
                                                            2002005356

♾™ The paper used in this publication meets the minimum requirements of American National Standard for Information Sciences—Permanence of Paper for Printed Library Materials, ANSI/NISO Z39.48-1992.
Manufactured in the United States of America.

Contents

Foreword		v
Preface		vii
Introduction: The Basic Argument		xi
1	What Counts in Accountability?	1
2	The Reliance on Standardized Special Event Testing	7
3	The Rap against Standardized Testing	13
4	Standardized Means Interpretable	19
5	Which Comes First, the Curriculum or the Test?	25
6	Hyping Student Performance Via the Cram Curriculum	29
7	What Ever Happened to the Scholastic Aptitude Test?	35
8	Avoiding the Information Age: The Road Not Considered	41
9	National Attention to Content and Performance Standards	47
10	Teacher Knows Best: Standardizing Teacher Judgment	57
11	Envisioning an Instructional Management Information System	61
12	How an Instructional Management Information System Would Work	65
13	Providing a Truly "Public" Education via the Internet	69
14	Rubrics and Grades: Getting Around the Curve	75

15 A New Credential: Certified Instructional Manager 85

16 By-Product I: New Information for College Admissions 89

17 By-Product II: Making Academics Count in the Workplace 93

18 A 21st Century Federal Initiative in Education 99

Epilogue 105

Index 111

About the Author 115

Foreword

This is a book that is long overdue. Finally, someone who understands the ins and outs of standardized, high-stakes testing has stepped forward with a practical and sound approach to the use of those tests in meeting educational standards. George Elford places the teacher, the student, and the local school curriculum at the center of the education and measurement process—which is where they belong. What he proposes is not "pie-in-the-sky" or empty rhetoric. His analysis is real; his approach is practical; and his recommendations are entirely doable.

In this interesting and informative book, Dr. Elford never takes his eye off the most critical element in evaluating student performance—the judgment of the teacher. That is refreshing, particularly in these days of state and federal government's infatuation with standardized tests (all too frequently aimed at attaining political rather than educational ends). His approach is particularly sanguine because in the pantheon of standardized testing, the judgment and interaction of the teacher is mostly ignored in the misleading allure of quick fix standardized tests.

Elford proposes that teacher involvement go in tandem with innovative, computer-based information systems designed to assist teachers in assessing student performance based on the school's curricula. He very accurately points out that when it comes to school management and accountability, American technology is not only shamefully underutilized; it is not even available to most teachers. He makes the convincing case that proper assessment tools and good information systems, combined with sound teacher judgment, will result in teaching, learning, and assessing that is far more productive. He proposes to harness the runaway horse of external standardized testing and move accountability where it belongs—internally to the local level.

This shift is to be accomplished through the development and utilization of computer-based instructional information systems that are based on the school's content and performance standards. This approach provides a thoughtful new perspective that focuses on education and learning rather than polls and instant political gratification.

To repeat, this book is long overdue. *Beyond Standardized Testing: Better Information for Accountability and School Management* offers hope for classroom teaches, students, and parents who are increasingly overwhelmed and frustrated as they valiantly try to respond to the increasing glut of external standardized tests that cascade relentlessly down upon them. George Elford not only offers hope for these folks, but he makes a significant contribution to the public debate about standards, testing, and accountability in education.

Don Cameron
Executive Director
National Education Association
1983–2001

Preface

Following the tragic events of September 11, 2001, the United States unleashed its technologically advanced military forces against terrorist Taliban forces then controlling Afghanistan. As this campaign moved ahead, the same United States was debating in Congress a test-based reform bill to improve American schools, another national priority.

In a *Washington Post* article entitled "An Education Plan with the Right Goal, Wrong Yardstick," Thomas Toch described the test-based reform plan with rigid standards as being "as ill-conceived as it was well-intentioned."[1] He cited research that suggested that 98 percent of the schools would flunk the Senate's standard and 100 percent would flunk the House's standard. These standards called for constant improvement in external standardized test scores for individual schools and for every sub-group within those schools. This, of course, is not how this kind of testing works. As Toch described it, legislators saw themselves with the choice of having these tough standards or appearing to join the anti-testing, anti-accountability advocates.

The juxtaposition of America's response to terrorism and the debate on testing shows the contrast between the advanced information technology serving the military and the nearly complete absence of information technology serving educators. The contrast is appalling! If the military were at the same level of technology as the schools, we would turn on our TV's to watch an attack on the Taliban by U.S. Marines hurling boulders using catapults.

What is even more remarkable than this stark contrast between the information technologies of the military and the technologies in schools is that the contrast has never been noticed? No one even suggested that the lack of information technology for school management and accountability was the real challenge facing Congress or anyone else seeking to improve America's schools.

The persistent interest in school reform has not been matched by an equally compelling vision of what a "reformed school" should look like. One vision reveals hours devoted to prepping students to take external standardized tests. If this is the vision of the future and the end result of "school reform," it is indeed a depressing vision and a sad result—more a nightmare than a vision! This book proposes a brighter vision for the future, a vision that sees beyond the current preoccupation with external standardized testing to the riches of the information age.

The vision offered in these pages has been fostered by my own experience and reflections from nearly 20 years of hands-on work with schools and assessments in the now defunct field services division of the Educational Testing Service (ETS). The vision builds on promising new developments that point to a new and better direction, including a renewed interest in content and performance standards and new assessment tools such as rubrics and protocols that give structure and support to teacher judgment.

A key to this new vision is the development of a comprehensive instructional management information system that both supports "standardized" teacher judgments and uses such judgments as the central component of a new accountability system. The new accountability system, which would be school-based rather than state-based, embraces and preserves these promising new developments, which could be lost unless incorporated into a new infrastructure created by such an information system.

External standardized testing as the present instrument of school reform, accountability, and college admissions is "special event testing," for which students are prepped and primed. Taking special event tests can be compared to taking the annual class picture or senior pictures from which results are received later. By embracing the Information Age, educators can move beyond these special, staged pictures to something analogous to instant snapshots or even streaming video. This move would be from a posed, staged event with results seen only later to real-time assessments with immediate results.

Readers will find that this book is about moving beyond standardized, special event testing to a new kind of assessment and information system. My goal is to raise the aspiration level of educational leaders and the public to demand the kind of instructional information that is readily possible with the information technology already on hand. The tools and remedies currently being embraced in the name of educational reform are quite obsolete and counterproductive, in contrast to what is now possible, given a networked computer on every teacher's desk.

The vision proposed here is a conservative one. There is no prediction of the end of schooling as we know it. The vision offered calls for a few simple changes in schools that will make profound differences. What I propose is not something akin to "Star Wars." It is something more akin to the idea of rural electrification when it was first proposed.

The book presents 18 chapters that can be read as separate pieces. Together these chapters argue for moving beyond traditional standardized or special event testing into the information age.

This book has benefited greatly from the assistance and encouragement of a number of people. Dorothy, my wife and in-house Internet expert, and my two daughters, Maura and Helene, were constant in their encouragement. My niece, Ellen Nagy, drew upon her experience as a pediatric nurse for information used in chapter 4. George Powell, Penelope Engel, and Janet Williams, former ETS colleagues, gave me help at important times. Tony Etienne, late of the Warsaw Indiana public schools, shared with me his encouraging view from "the trenches." The librarians at the Montgomery County (MD) Public Schools Professional Library were most helpful on numerous occasions.

George W. Elford
Potomac, Maryland
January 2002

NOTE

1. Thomas Toch, "An Education Plan with the Right Goal, Wrong Yardstick," *The Washington Post* 18 Nov. 2001: B5.

Introduction: The Basic Argument

Schooling in America is suffering serious negative consequences from a preoccupation with external standardized testing for admissions and accountability purposes. This "special event testing" has given rise to the "cram curriculum," and test-based reform is turning schools into test-prep centers with unfortunate effects. Standardized tests are designed primarily to create summary descriptive statistics based on student responses to questions in an artificial context. These secondary sources of information on learning are consuming public attention and resources. As a result, teachers in the classroom, who daily observe the actual work of students, are overlooked as the primary and richest source of information on learning. Teachers are out of the loop for want of an information system that puts a computer on every teacher's desk.

The practical answer is not to attack standardized testing, which supplies the only interpretable information the public has been able to attain. The answer is to look beyond standardized testing and into the information age, which has barely reached schools. The answer is to create a school- and teacher-based instructional management information system that gives more and better information and in turn serves accountability defined more broadly. Such comprehensive, computer based systems would link every teacher and classroom into their school district's data warehouse. The system would support and utilize the richest source of accountability information, the presently untapped knowledge in the minds of teachers.

At the heart of the system would be "standardized teacher judgments" related to content and performance standards and using standards-based scoring rubrics. To be effective and extensively used in schools, scoring rubrics would have to be integrated into a computer-based instructional management information system. With such a use of rubrics, grading on the curve will disappear. Students will be graded on the quality of their work and not on how they compare to other students.

With the resources of an instructional management information system at their fingertips, teachers will be able to record "standardized judgments" on the performance of their students. These "standardized judgments" will attain the status of objective data that had heretofore been reserved to the results of standardized tests. As a richer and more timely source of objective data, these teacher judgments will better fit the bill for accountability and reduce the demand for external standardized testing.

This new information system would make the school or school district the primary source of accountability information, instead of the state. It would create a virtually new field of expertise, school-based instructional management and, possibly, an important new, performance-based credential (Certified Instructional Manager). It would provide better information for college admissions and a record for employers that would show the link between school and work.

The technology for such a system is currently available and continues to become more available, with the advent of wireless networks, although attention and effort are not expended in this volume on recommending a specific technology. Endorsements of existing hardware would quickly make this work out of date. Besides, the expertise available on relevant information technology is close to overwhelming. The focus here is on the urgent need for a computer-based instructional information system to which every teacher is linked.

The creation of such a generic system would be an appropriate 21st century role for federal government, which could be tasked to develop a generic software authoring package for an information system with which each school could carry out and report on its own standards-based program. The federal government would become a major contributor to significant reform for schools of all kinds, enabling each school to better attain its own self-determined mission and standards.

1

What Counts in Accountability?

The demand for accountability drives the current emphasis on standardized, special event testing administered by external agencies. These tests are most often county or state assessments and college admissions tests. Often discussed national testing would be another in this list of external tests. Accountability is the demand for evidence that the schools are working effectively and that students are learning the skills they need. Accountability is the search for a balance sheet to describe the academic prosperity or bankruptcy of a school.

The focus of accountability is more the schools than it is the students. Families are the principal locus of accountability for individual students as they bring home their reports cards. Grades are still the standards that mostly affect student performance and parental views. In school accountability, however, grades and conduct are overlooked. The accountability that currently drives the demand for external testing has the school as the focus of concern. Schools must attain certain standards in terms of the percent of students attaining certain scores. Schools that fail to meet these standards are singled out for corrective actions.

REGIONAL ACCREDITATION: THE MAGINOT LINE

Decades ago, educational leaders prepared the schools for a certain kind of accountability. They put in place an elaborate system to address challenges that questioned the academic quality of their schools. They established and have for decades operated an "assessment system" to document the quality of schools and to assure the public that their schools meet quality standards. They put in place systems of regional accreditation with regional voluntary associations, such as the North Central Association of Schools and Colleges, which serves the Midwest. Each region has its own regional accrediting association, and in each region, educators from schools and colleges adopt standards of quality that member schools have agreed to attain to make each school "creditable," i.e., able to award valid credits that other schools will accept. These standards focused almost entirely on inputs and processes, such as teacher credentials, school facilities, access to learning materials, well-defined and implemented policies and procedures, etc. On a periodic schedule (say every five years) each member school, seeking to renew its accreditation, would conduct an internal review or self-study of its compliance with the association's standards.

With this self-study in hand, a visiting team of educators selected by the accrediting body would then conduct a formal and extended visit to the school and meet with the staff. They would then file a report to the accrediting body with recommendations either that the school be approved or placed on probation pending certain changes. This has been a serious process, which presumably has had positive effects on U.S. schools. It has been the credentialing process that was intended to assure the public they have quality schools.

Regional accreditation was expected to serve as the line of defense in case of any attack that questioned the quality of America's schools. In this regard, regional accreditation calls to mind the elaborate set of defenses called the Maginot Line, which France built after World War I to protect its territory against a German invasion. When the invasion finally did come, the German army simply went around the Maginot Line. In some ways, this has happened to the regional accreditation process. In response to challenges to the quality of U.S. schools and the demand for accountability, it was not enough to point to the framed certificate of accreditation hanging in the school's office.

With its focus on inputs, processes and procedures, regional accreditation has been largely ignored in the search for a school accountability balance sheet. Pollsters have not even asked the public or the business community whether they have confidence in U.S. schools, since after all they are accredited. Registrars value accreditation in their acceptance of educational credit from other schools. The demand for accountability has led people to look beyond accreditation for hard data on what students know and can do.

Though publicly ignored, regional accreditation has left its mark on some formulations of accountability. The National Center for Educational Outcomes, for example, has developed a framework for accountability[1] (that reflects the influence of the accreditation process. They developed "outcomes and indicators" for six levels of education from pre-school to "post-school" in the following three categories: educational inputs and resources, educational processes, and educational results. They have rescued much of the accreditation effort and now call it accountability.

While the Center does include educational results, they avoid a narrow focus on academic learning. The domains covered under educational results include: academic and functional literacy, physical health, responsibility and independence, citizenship, personal and social well-being and satisfaction. Possessing a good self-image is, of course, part of personal and social well-being. However, such a sweepingly broad and "soft" conceptualization of accountability will not answer today's demand for "hard data" accountability.

TEST-BASED ACCOUNTABILITY

A hard data approach to accountability is exemplified in California's Academic Performance Index (API), a first step in the development of a comprehensive accountability system for California public schools. The API uses an externally developed standardized test (Stanford 9) that "measures overall student performance at every school and places every school on a scale of 200 to 1000 with a state-defined target score (currently 800). The API assessments in grades 2–8 cover four content areas, which are weighted in their contribution to the single index score. They are weighted as follows: mathematics (40%), reading (30%), language (15%) and spelling (15%).

Schools, having set their growth targets each year in terms of this index, are compared with schools statewide and with schools with similar demographics. This is closer to what the temper of the times seems to demand for accountability. This is California's approach, although there are as many approaches as there are states. The common element in all of these approaches is dependence on external standardized testing, using a technology that dates back to the mid-twentieth century.

IMPORTANT ACCOUNTABILITY QUESTIONS

The accountability movement, unfortunately, has framed its questions to elicit the answers that current test data can provide. The movement has overlooked the potential new resources created by the advent of the information age and the universal availability of computers. These make it possible to answer more important questions.

What kind of accountability questions should be raised and answered? Significant accountability questions seldom, if ever, addressed, include the following:

- In terms of performance standards, what is the school trying to accomplish grade by grade? On which standards are teachers in the classrooms spending their time? What are the principal performance standards for each grade as identified by the teachers themselves?
- How would the teachers rate their students in terms of their mastery of these performance standards using standardized rating scales?
- What other internal or external assessment data describe the students' attainment of these same standards? How well are the students learning what the school is trying to teach?
- How, as a group, do "A" students, "B" students, etc. do on each of the performance standards? Do the grades makes sense in terms of what students are able to do? What does it mean to be an "A" student at this school?

For example, Figure 1.1 shows the picture one would expect for a school where grades in general made sense.

In the above fictional sample, it was assumed that grading is not perfect and that "D" and "F" students have conduct and attendance problems that also shape their grades.

If schools could routinely answer these questions for the community they serve, the accountability demands would be met by the local schools. The focus would then shift from the state to the local school as the source of accountability information.

Many years ago, in my fieldwork with ETS, I had occasion to show in a workshop for school administrators a table in which standardized achievement test scores were matched with course grades in the same subject. The participants were astonished and excited. They were also quite pleased. The picture made sense. The workshop that day was on setting standards or passing scores on minimum competency tests. The display suggested that the average score of "D" students matched the passing scores identified from other standard-setting methods. The broad range in the "D" scores also showed some very able "D" students who earned their

Figure 1.1

Standard #1 Students will read and understand middle school reading materials.

Ratings by Teachers for Students Grouped By Course Grades (%)

	Advanced	Proficient	Basic	N
Grades Awarded				
A students	85	15	0	65
B students	5	80	15	90
C students	0	10	75*	68
D students	0	5	60*	20
F students	0	0	40*	5

* the remaining % of students were rated as below the basic level

"D" presumably for non-academic reasons. These finer points were overshadowed by the larger message that grades and test scores should be looked at side by side, something that is almost never done.

This simple display was a picture these educators had seldom seen before or since. It was also a picture one would expect to be a standard piece in educational reporting. That picture very graphically displayed the academic standards of that school district better than any average scores. The standards of a school are not created by the average scores of their students but by the manner in which the faculty evaluates (grades) student work. For example, School X with many able students could have high average test scores. It also could have inflated grading standards, with the result that much work School X graded with an "A" would be graded with a "B" in School Y, which may have fewer able students and lower average test scores. Accountability in the information age should focus on the standards of the school as much on the average scores of its students.

The same information systems that could give these enriched accountability reports would also create for the first time the database needed for the hands-on management of instruction at the each school.

NOTE

1. National Center For Educational Outcomes at www.coled.umn.edu/ NCEO

2

The Reliance on Standardized Special Event Testing

My first recollections of standardized testing date to the 1940s, when I was in grade school. Every year or so, we would take a battery of achievement tests, for which there was absolutely no fanfare or pressure to prepare. The idea in this kind of testing was to take an unposed snapshot of student achievement, an objective that guided the use of standardized testing for many years when the uses of the test results were largely academic.

Years later, in my field work with ETS, school districts often requested help with figuring out how to use their test results. They had invested time and money in these tests and were looking for a greater return. The underutilization of test results was a long-standing complaint with standardized testing in those years. By this time in the 1970s, standardized tests were required as part of the program evaluations for the Federal Title I programs funded by the 1965 legislation called the Elementary and Secondary Education Act (ESEA).

Even with these added uses, state mandated standardized testing for Title I still had not evolved into the phenomenon of special event testing that we see today. The only special event tests in those days were college admissions, tests such as the SAT and the ACT. Even for these tests, specialized preparation only gradually became the rule, as these tests came to be viewed as life-defining events. Stanley Kaplan expanded his test prep services over several decades into the 1980s, at which point Princeton Review entered the booming field as an aggressive competitor.

STATE ASSESSMENTS: READY AND WAITING

In the late 1960s, states began to develop their own state assessments, thus beginning a movement that grew steadily in subsequent years. Some states developed their own tests with committees of teachers and supervisors, while others adopted commercially developed tests. In the early decades of this movement, tests of this type were not viewed as special events for which special preparation or notice was expected. The state assessment movement, however, grew to the extent that, when accountability came front and center on the national agenda, state assessments were ready and waiting in the wings.

As Kathy Doherty has reported in *Education Week,* the states that had not previously joined the movement, rapidly did so, with the result that by 2001 all 50 states had state assessments.[1] Forty-nine states use tests with multiple-choice questions, and 38 include short-answer questions. Many states use writing samples to assess writing skills, and seven states have open-ended assessment in other subjects as well. Two states use portfolio assessments, which include an array of student work.

That standardized testing has quickly become the centerpiece in accountability and school reform efforts for a number of reasons pointed out by the noted testing expert, Robert Linn. He observed that:

- Tests are relatively inexpensive compared to other reform efforts such as attracting better teachers, providing significant professional development for teachers, etc.
- Tests can be externally mandated at the state or district level much more easily than significant changes in the classroom can be identified and mandated.
- New tests can be implemented in a short time, within the term of an elected official. Test results are visible. They can be reported in the press. They often show bad news, which makes good copy.[2]

Standardized testing thus easily rises to the top of the list of politically viable, rapid responses to the demand "to do something about our schools." It fits all the requirements of a quick fix.

In an era of test-based accountability, the public image or description of any local school is based entirely on state assessment results. Interested people can now go to the Internet for information about local schools. There they will find their school described entirely in terms of state assessment results, the only information ready for use by the web-site developer.

ACCOUNTABILITY VIA STATE ASSESSMENTS

State assessment people have developed an imaginative array of schemata for presenting their results. As noted earlier, California uses it own Academic Performance Index, which is a weighted composite set of results from math and language arts testing. Each school has its own index score and a ranking statewide and a ranking with schools of similar demographics. One school, for example, had a lower index score and statewide ranking (6) but a high score within its group ranking (9). In such cases, as Robert Linn noted,[3] some educators will call attention to their within-group ranking and downplay their index score. Within-group rankings could evolve into lower standards for schools serving the disadvantaged.

Florida has developed a system for grading schools from A to F using a very complex set of standards for each grade interval. For example, grades of A or B require a certain level of attainment by all the students and by subgroups on the Florida Comprehensive Assessment Test (FCAT) against a higher set of performance criteria. Grades of C, D, and F are awarded on more minimum criteria and fewer requirements. In Florida, schools get ratings that call to mind Standard and Poor's ratings of bonds.

North Carolina uses a reporting system that focuses on growth from the previous year. They use the average rate of growth observed across the state from one year to the next as the benchmark that creates the expected gain for all of the schools as shown on the state assessment. They then place schools in one of four categories based on the school's rate of gain. In 1999–2000, 45 percent of the schools were exemplary in the gains they reported, while 24 percent made the expected or average gain. Some 30 percent failed to meet the gain standard. Unfortunately, the pattern in schooling is that the educationally rich get richer and the poor get poorer. Not all students are "flat-liners" when it comes to score gain over time. The trend lines for the better students go up steadily, and the trend lines for the poorer students go steadily downward. Better students tend to show greater gains and poorer students less gain.

The Tennessee Value–Added Assessment System (4) ranks as the most sophisticated accountability system in use. It uses a sophisticated data-analysis methodology in its analysis of student gains that creates data for looking at the performance of teachers, schools, and districts over several years.

The upshot of all of these various systems of assessment and reporting is that the local school is out of the information stream. School staff are not asked to provide their own information about how well their school is doing. Those answers come from the state assessment people. For purposes of accountability, it is the state that keeps the accounts.

One result of these new accountability reports that rank schools is especially valuable. These rankings reinforce the silent system of public school choice that has worked effectively for American public schools for decades. Public schools are used far more extensively than other public services. Affluent and middle class Americans feel comfortable using nearby public schools but would not think of going to a public hospital or a public home for the aged. People of means spend not just to meet basic needs but to attain and preserve social differentiation. Public schools through real estate markets provide for differentiation. Affluent people can happily use their public schools because, on the charts now published in the accountability effort, their schools are clearly differentiated and shown to be top schools. Real estate agents are the effective operators of this silent choice system. They now have added information on elementary and middle schools along with additional high school information to supplement the college admissions test scores and rankings they have used for years.

SOME LIMITATIONS WITH STATE ASSESSMENTS

A question that arises with state assessments as used for accountability is whether these assessments are describing the school and its program or simply its students. A school that begins the year with 90 percent excellent students is most likely to end the year with test results showing 90 percent of the students as excellent. Is this school's program that much better than a school that began with 50 percent excellent students and ended at the same level? If you look at the percent of mastery in these schools, the one with 90 percent excellent students at the start will always look better.

State assessments are aerial views of the school; they do not get into the classrooms. A constant rejoinder from teachers about state assessments is that the tests do not cover what they are teaching. In a ten-state study, Wisconsin researchers found little overlap between the state assessments and what teachers actually taught. In one state, the overlap

Figure 2.1

A Sample of NAEP Reporting By Levels of Skill

Level of Skill in Writing	% of Students
Can write effective responses with details and discussion	2
Can write complete responses with sufficient information	31
Can begin to write focused and clear responses to tasks	83
Can write partial or vague responses	99

in one subject was only 5 percent.[5] Any true assessment of a school must address what is now the great unknown, what are the teachers teaching behind their closed doors? A well-designed information system that begins with a computer on every teacher's desk will answer this fundamental question.

Another limitation with state assessments as the primary provider of information for accountability is that they give only the kinds of scores and information that multiple-choice tests can give. These kinds of assessments usually do not directly tell us what students can and cannot do. Such reports are forthcoming from another source. The National Assessment of Educational Progress (NAEP) not long ago introduced a dramatic improvement in the reporting of assessment results. Their reports directly address the question of what students can and cannot do at various age/grade levels. Figure 2.1 presents, as an example, a 1996 grade 11 report on writing skills.

This incorporation of performance levels into assessment reporting was, in my view, the most significant breakthrough in assessment reporting in decades. The reason is that such an approach gives parents and employers the kind of information they can understand and use. In the information age, this is the kind of information schools should be able to give to parents and their local communities about what the schools are attempting to do and what, as a result, can students do or not do.[6]

An unfortunate result of the pre-eminence of state assessments is that whatever interest there may be in building new capabilities in information technology, the attention is likely to be directed toward the state rather than the local schools where the business of teaching and learning is carried out.

NOTES

1. Kathy Doherty, "Assessment," *Education Week* 16, July 2001.
2. Robert Linn, 1995 ETS Angoff Lecture, Educational Testing Service, Princeton, N. J.
3. Robert Linn, "Reporting School Quality in Standards-Based Accountability Systems, CREST Policy Brief 3," National Center for Research on Evaluation, Standards, and Student Testing, Spring 2001, www.cse.ucla.edu
4. Robert Linn, op cit.
5. Ulrich Boser, "Teaching to the Test," *Education Week* 7, June 2000.
6. "National Assessment of Educational Progress (NAEP) 1996 Trends in Academic Progress," National Center for Educational Statistics, 1997, www.asbj.com/evs/97/commonmeasures.html

3

The Rap against Standardized Testing

The pervasive use of external standardized testing in the multiple-choice format in the pursuit of accountability has not been without its critics. The critics of such testing object to the following dimensions of the tests:

- they are external and not classroom based
- they are multiple choice and not performance based.

Other, admittedly infrequent, uses of standardized multiple-choice tests by classroom teachers or departments within local schools are not subject to criticism. Likewise, the use of standardized methodologies for essay scoring or the scoring of portfolio contents such as book reports, lab reports, etc. also is exempt from criticism.

RAPS AGAINST EXTERNAL STANDARDIZED TESTING

Here are the usual raps against external standardized testing in the multiple-choice format.

- **Overuse of a single score.** This criticism harks back to one of the cardinal principles of test use that calls for test scores to be used, if at all possible, with other data in making any decisions. This criticism has gained in frequency and gravity with the exclusive use of test scores in many accountability schemes. Exaggerating the importance of a single test score creates the phenomenon of special event testing. This, in turn, causes teachers and students to invest time and resources to generate an atypical performance for this staged look at the students' abilities.

- **People who do not do well on tests.** Critics of standardized tests cite the number of good students who do not do well on external, special event tests or standardized tests. This number has never been quantified. Evidence here is personal and anecdotal. Presumably, this phenomenon is a result of the extra stress associated with special event, timed testing that does not affect these same students in a classroom test or final exam.
- **Overemphasis on factual recall.** Critics identify multiple-choice questions with the assessment of only factual knowledge or "factoids." There is a serious gravitational pull toward the assessment of factual knowledge in the construction of multiple-choice questions. Easy-to-write items always test factual recall. Tests developed in-house by companies or units of the military include factual recall questions almost exclusively. Numbers, names, terms, etc., attract less than expert test questions writers. There are, however, examples of multiple-choice questions that test reasoning. One prominent national test gives the test-takers the facts needed to answer the question and asks the test-taker to identify the salient facts and to apply them in what is a demonstration of reasoning skills.
- **The "Inauthentic" Character of Multiple-Choice Testing.** Critics assail multiple-choice testing as not representative of the desired outcomes of schooling. Students are sent to school to master a range of skills that enable them to do certain things such as reading, thinking, analyzing, problem solving, and writing in various forms. Having students actually do these kinds of things is held up as the most desirable test for students. Multiple-choice tests of writing skills have garnered the most criticism. Performance assessments in the form of actual written exercises have become commonplace in assessment programs in response to these criticisms. The Advanced Placement tests in a host of subject fields are standardized tests that have escaped most criticism because they include essay or open-ended questions as well as multiple-choice questions. These tests combine the richness of open-ended questions with the breadth of coverage and the reliability of multiple-choice questions.
- **A Flawed Meritocracy.** Critics of standardized college admissions testing lament the prospect that the ruling class in the United States will be a meritocracy shaped by successful performance on a single measure of aptitude, on which the already advantaged tend to do well. This criticism challenges the position of testing companies that argue that

college admissions testing opens doors to less advantaged students. The critics argue their position on the basis of averages. Advantaged students on average outscore the disadvantaged. Lurking behind these averages are, however, significant numbers of advantaged students who do not do that well and a number of disadvantaged students who do quite well. This argument has limited appeal. The public tends to be comfortable with the idea of people who do well on standardized tests advancing in the learned professions, such as medicine and law.

- **Disadvantaging Minority Students.** Another criticism of multiple-choice, standardized testing is that these tests are disadvantageous to minority students, who on average do less well that non-minority students. The problem with this criticism is that on performance assessments, the alternative to multiple-choice testing, these same differences either persist or are greater. In some cases, external standardized tests are set up for a fall with minority students. Studies have shown a pattern in which some minority students are highly praised and given high marks for what is, in fact, mediocre work. These students and their parents then are shocked to see their comparatively poor results on a norm-referenced standardized test. All in all, one could safely say that the educational problems of minority students do not result from standardized testing.
- **Cultural Bias in Testing.** For the most part, standardized, multiple-choice tests are culturally biased in favor of the "culture" toward which the test is directed. For example, college admissions tests favor students most at home with the spoken and written language used in college classrooms and textbooks. I once saw on television a clip in which a college professor was attacking the SAT and telling his class about the cultural bias in the SAT. In his lecture, he used words like "argot," which would appear to be favored by students who do well on the SAT. Some test critics have developed tests of "street-wiseness" on which minorities do better than advantaged non-minority students. These examples simply make the case that cultural bias can cut different ways. The validity of a test is established when it is shown that the test measures what it purports to measure as expressed in the name of the test. If either the SAT or the test of "street-wiseness" were labeled tests of native intelligence, both would be invalid. As measures of scholastic aptitude or "street-wiseness" both are indeed valid, despite their cultural bias identified by the name on the test cover.

- **Fragmentation of Knowledge.** A trenchant critic of multiple-choice standardized testing is Jacques Barzun, who sees such testing as focused on recognition knowledge, "knowledge at the far side of the memory, where shapes are dim." These tests address "only passive recognition-knowledge, not active usable knowledge." As Barzun notes,

- Knowing something—really knowing it—means being able to summon it out of the blue; the facts must be produced in their right relations and with their correct significance.
- ... The worst feature of this game of choosing the ready-made instead of producing the fresh idea is that it breaks up the unity of what has been learned and isolates the pieces.
- ... True testing issues a call for patterns, and this is the virtue of the essay examination. Both preparing for it and taking it reinforce the pattern originally formed, and degrees of ability show themselves not in the number of lucky hits, but in the scope, coherence, and verbal accuracy of each whole answer.[1]

Barzun then sees schools setting up "courses in thinking" for students who have been made "cripples in consecutive thought."

In the wake of the above criticisms of multiple-choice standardized tests, some agencies have switched from the multiple-choice format in which the student identifies the correct answer to a fill-in-the-blank format in which the student must supply the answer. For example, here is the same question in the two formats:

Who was the third president of the United States?

  A. John Adams
  B. Thomas Jefferson
  C. James Madison
  D. James Monroe

The third president of the United States was _____.

While the fill-in-the-blank format tends to be slightly more difficult, it nonetheless poses the same kind of recall question. In many cases, the efficiency in the machine scoring of multiple-choice questions offsets the increased difficulty of the question. The move to performance assessment is more convincingly attained by posing questions that go beyond simple recall.

Drawing on various combinations and weightings of the above raps against standardized testing, a steady stream of criticism of standardized testing has continued for several decades. This stream of criticism gave rise in the late 1970s to an organized attack on standardized testing and particularly the SAT. A catalyst in this attack was Ralph Nader, who saw ETS as the General Motors of testing. College student members of Nader's Public Interest Research Groups (PIRGs) were the foot soldiers bringing this attack to over 30 state legislatures and the U.S. Congress. The target in this effort was the passage of "Truth in Testing" legislation, which called for test companies to publish their secure tests after they were administered. The passage of such a bill in New York in 1979 alleviated the need for its passage elsewhere. There was never a large demand for this new test disclosure among students. The major consumers for this disclosure service proved to be those interested in the launching of a golden age for the test prep industry.

POLLS FAVOR TESTING

This attack on standardized testing and the SAT never took the form of a direct, frontal assault designed to end such testing—a goal that was never politically feasible. While many in the movement would have welcomed such an outcome, the attack had to be limited to tinkering around the edges, because of continuous public endorsement of standardized testing, which has been backed by poll data showing consistent popular support. With standardized tests as the centerpiece in the states' accountability plans, this consistent level of support remains evident in the polls. In a January 2001 Gallup poll,[2] people were asked to rate several proposals for improving public schools by answering a question in the following format: "Would this proposal improve public schools a great deal, a fair amount, not much, or not at all?" Concerning the proposal to use "standardized tests to hold schools accountable," 38 percent saw this as helping "a great deal," and 35 percent saw them helping a "fair amount." Only nine percent saw this as "not helping at all." Another poll at this same time asked if students in public schools should be required to pass a standardized test in order to be promoted the next level?[3] Some 77 percent answered yes, they should.

This consistent public support for one source of information, namely standardized multiple-choice testing, could be affected by the absence of other comparable sources of information. Interpretable information is what is popular. Multiple-choice standardized tests are now seen as the only source of such information. Other sources of dependable educational information are nowhere in evidence in education today, despite the awesome developments of the information age. The information technology of the mid-twentieth century, represented by machine-scored, computer tallied standardized tests remains for now, the predominant and almost sole information technology in U.S. schools.

In contrast to the paper-intensive, batch-processing approach now used with standardized testing, consider the technology used by the leased car inspector who came to inspect my about-to-be-returned leased car. All of his information and comments were quickly entered into a hand held computer. He then plugged the hand-held computer into a computer and printer in the backseat of his car and gave me two copies of his report. There are probably 10,000 teachers observing the work and performance of students for every inspector of leased cars. Why don't teachers have the same level of technology at their service that these car inspectors have?

Multiple-choice standardized testing suffers the most from overuse, as the only game in town. People would likely embrace a better vision, if they had a chance. The same polls valued school-based information as more important than external standardized tests. When asked which was the best way to measure student achievement, 68 percent selected "classroom work and homework" and 26 percent selected tests.[4] In another sequence asking the best way to measure achievement, 13 percent selected "a single standardized test," 41 percent selected "a combination of standardized and teacher-made tests," and portfolios of student work and other demonstrations of attainment.[5] People are looking for better information more closely tied to the teacher in the classroom. In this information age, we need to develop the kind of instructional information system that will meet this demand and take the excessive pressure off external standardized testing.

NOTES

1. Jacques Barzun, *Begin Here: The Forgotten Conditions of Teaching and Learning*, Chicago: University of Chicago Press, 1991, pp. 33–35.
2. Gallup Poll Topics: A-Z Education, The Gallup Organization, www.gallup.com/poll/indicators/indeducation.asp
3. Frank Newport, "Americans Strongly Behind Mandatory School Testing" The Gallup Organization, Poll Analyses, August 2, 2001, www.gallup.com/poll/releases/pr010802.asp
4. Ibid.
5. Ibid.

4

Standardized Means Interpretable

Within minutes of their birth, newborn infants are greeted with their first standardized test. The physician or nurse uses the Apgar Observational Rating Scale to rate and assign a number value to the infant's responsiveness and basic functioning. This numerical rating is entered into the infant's medical record. The top score is a perfect ten. Scores at or below seven call for special attention. Other medical personnel looking at this record will understand what the physician or nurse observed in those early minutes because the Apgar scale is standardized. If each physician used his or her own way of rating an infant on these specific dimensions, only that physician would know what his/her rating meant. Having the rating scale standardized makes it widely interpretable. Note also that the end product of the rating process is a number, a summary statistic.

In response to the predominance of standardized testing in schools, some educators have promoted, as an alternative, portfolios of student papers that had been reviewed and graded. Unfortunately, what needed to be collected were not the papers themselves but understandable judgments or ratings about the quality of these papers. From aggregated ratings can come the kind of summary statistics needed for better accountability and instructional management. The Apgar scale is a simple but instructive example of "standardized" ratings aggregated into a summary statistic.

WHAT IS STANDARDIZATION?

A standardized measure is one that is administered under uniform conditions and is scored according to well-defined scoring procedures. In many cases, including the APGAR scales, the training of raters or scorers is

required. The goal of standardization is to produce results or scores that are interpretable by people not involved in the assessment.
The elements that make a test standardized are the following:

1. Directions for administering the test are specific, so that all students complete the test under the same conditions.
2. The scoring of the test is administered uniformly, so that pre-defined scoring procedures are implemented consistently. Many of these are machine scored. Scorers are, as a rule, trained in the scoring of open-ended tests.
3. The above conditions create the assumption of objectivity in the test results that gives standardized measures their value for accountability purposes.
4. The nature, content and purpose of the test are clearly defined so that the test actually measures what it purports to measure (validity).
5. The test is of sufficient length and quality so that students' scores would not be very different if they took a parallel form of the test the next day (reliability).

Standardization does not mean that national or other norms are used for reporting results. Standardized tests can be either norm-referenced or criterion-referenced or both. A norm-referenced test reports results in terms of how the students performed in comparison to the performance of the sample of students who took the test as a part of a norming study. A percentile, for example, is a norm-referenced statistic that describes where students scored in terms of the percent of the norm group who scored below them. A student at the 80th percentile scored better than 80 percent of the norm group.

The samples of students in national norming studies are selected randomly and are not prepped in any way. Norms are used for a number of years due to the high costs of norming studies. In the late 1980s a West Virginia physician discovered that all 32 states that used normed-references tests were above average, like the students in the mythical Lake Wobegon. As a result of various efforts at test prepping and curriculum alignment, these schools were able to "beat" the scores of the un-prepped norm group. The result was that some 70 percent of the students were above average. This became known as the "Lake Wobegone phenomenon." Any use of norm-referenced testing must pay careful attention to the norm group.

A criterion-referenced test is one in which the results are reported in reference to a standard or criterion. Such a test might, for example, report a student as excellent, proficient or needing improvement. Pass/fail tests are criterion referenced.

On most standardized tests, research is conducted to analyze the properties and effective functioning of the test in terms of how it relates to similar tests. Standardized tests in any form require an investment of time and expertise.

Most people use the term "standardized test" to refer to a nationally normed, machine-scored, paper and pencil test using multiple-choice questions. Some 125 million of these tests are administered annually in U.S. schools, and they are indeed standardized tests. Tests of this type are administered under defined and controlled conditions and with a pre-set scoring key loaded into the computer.

STANDARDIZED BUT NOT MULTIPLE-CHOICE ASSESSMENTS

A writing exercise, however, can also be a standardized assessment when all of the students respond to the same prompts under the same conditions and time constraints, and the students' writing is scored by trained readers using a pre-defined score scale. These score scales often come with sample papers at each of the score points to give the scorer an even clearer picture. When the scoring is completed, teachers familiar with the process will know the characteristics of an "8" paper and those of a "4" paper and the kinds of help the students will need.

One of the most highly regarded standardized assessment program is the Advanced Placement Program in which high school students, after taking an AP course in a specific subject, complete both a standardized examination with both a multiple choice and an open ended section. Trained readers using carefully defined scoring rubrics and sample papers for each scale point score the latter. The scoring system takes into account how college students, who have successfully completed a college course in the subject of the Advanced Placement examination, would score on this test. Colleges then may choose to award college credit to students whose scores match their standards. Hence the name "advanced placement."

Portfolio assessment has been touted as an important alternative to multiple-choice standardized assessments. A portfolio (as in portfolio assessment) is a file folder containing a collection of student work samples that students select for review to show the quality of work they are doing. The students furnish the criteria used in selecting these pieces and their own reflections on what the portfolio tells them about their progress. Most portfolio assessments find their value in the richness of the experience itself and their instructional usefulness and not in the hard data produced from this kind of assessment. These assessments tend to fall short of serving as standardized measures.

One of the most ambitious and promising ventures in standardization was ACT's development of the Passport Portfolio Program for secondary schools. ACT took steps to incorporate standardization and interpretability with this new program at the high school level. They quite shrewdly began by creating the concept of a "work sample" as a generic category or type of academic task that teachers assign in different courses at different levels in a general field such as language arts or mathematics. The tasks represent important elements in a school's curriculum. For example in language arts, the assigned tasks might include:

- Response to a literary text
- Research writing
- Review of arts or media
- Uses of language
- Short story/drama
- Poetry
- Personal experience
- Explanation/analysis
- Persuasive writing
- Business writing.

For each of these work samples or types of academic task, scoring protocols are developed to allow each task to be scored on a six-point scale. Teachers are clued into this assessment system to ensure they make a number of assignments across the entire array of tasks. Students would then have a significant number of papers from which to choose in assembling, say, their language arts portfolio each year. This system calls for portfolios to be assessed each of the four years of high school. ACT's Passport Portfolio program thus expands the horizon of standardized assessment to include portfolio assessments, which generate scores that are interpretable and comparable across years and across high schools. The program makes possible student recognition for scholarships and other awards based on the quality of the students' work in mastering a school's own curriculum.

STANDARDIZATION IN THE INFORMATION AGE

The advent of microcomputing has dramatically expanded the potential for effective new forms of standardized assessment within the classroom and the school's own curriculum. The micro- or laptop computer can give teachers the tools they need to observe and record in a structured, standardized format their students' mastery of the knowledge and skills covered in their curriculum. Computers with pull-down screens and branching could allow teachers to quickly review scoring rubrics and look at scored work samples as they rated their own students' attainment. What teachers could not completely retain in their heads would still be at their fingertips. With such first-hand knowledge they would be in a position to generate the best available information on what their students could and could not do. The information age has reached the classroom when the computers are on the teachers' desks in the schools!

5

Which Comes First, the Curriculum or the Test?

"Which comes first, the curriculum or the test?" There was a time in education when that question would never have been asked. Of course, the curriculum comes first. Tests are generated to assess student mastery of the curriculum. For decades, it was assumed that changing or reforming schools would begin with the curriculum and the teachers' readiness to teach that curriculum. The central focus in educational debate has been with the curriculum. The history of American education has been recorded in terms of a long-running struggle for control over the curriculum between the proponents of the subject-matter curriculum and the proponents of the life-experience curriculum. The curriculum is the school's raison d'etre. Both as a building and an organization, the school exists chiefly to deliver the curriculum.

Curriculum design begins with the identification of the needs of the students. The next steps are the formulation of objectives and the selection of content. In a work on curriculum evaluation, Robert Gagne pointed out that these are one and the same: "Content may be defined as descriptions of the expected capabilities in specified domains of human activity."[1] According to Gagne, content needs to be stated as objectives that are descriptions of what students are expected to be able to do following a particular period or unit of learning. In Gagne's words, "a curriculum is a sequence of content units arranged in such a way that the learning of each unit may be accomplished as a single act, provided the capabilities described by specified prior units in the sequence have already been mastered by the learner." A school's curriculum is not to be viewed as a casual happening. It is a thoughtful, well-developed plan for teaching and learning. By design, it must also address the need for assessing its own effectiveness. Any serious reform in schooling should focus on the curriculum and its implementation. Long-respected thinking in education tells us that is how it is supposed to be!

A CURRICULUM OVERRIDE

With the predominance of standardized testing in the reform movement and the absence of any useful public information about the schools' effectiveness with their own curriculum, external standardized testing has taken over. The schools' own curricula have been moved to the background. No one even talks about holding a school "accountable" for the successful implementation of its own curriculum.

One reason for this is schools, despite the information age, have no useful or interpretable information to share on how well the students are mastering their curriculum. Schools lack the information systems to develop the needed information from their own curriculum.

As a quick approach to educational reform, turning to external standardized tests at the expense of the schools' own curricula has definite appeal for a number of reasons. Evidence suggests that the implementation of a school's own curriculum may be overridden or reshaped by teachers' particular interests and their own take on what their students really need. The extent of this trend is difficult to document. Schools lack the internal information systems needed for effective instructional management. It could well be that principals know more about what is going on in the halls than what is going on in the classrooms after the teachers close their doors.

Students also can shape the implementation of a curriculum in their interaction with their teachers in the classroom. In what has been described by Theodore Sizer as "Horace's compromise," students can "negotiate" or pressure teachers into lowering expectations.[2] The students offer a deal: they will not make trouble if the teacher only requires so much and no more. In happy but probably rare instances, students can encourage teachers to demand more, when, for example, optional extra work is done by most of the students.

TEST-BASED REFORMS AS QUICK "SOLUTIONS"

For the test-based reformer, the external standardized test addresses both of these problems. Reformers see testing as giving a clearer focus to the work of both the teacher and the student. With the tests, according to the test-based reformers, is what teachers should teach and what students should learn.

Test-based reform is a fairly easy proposition. It is not terribly difficult to develop a quality test with interesting questions. It takes extensive and serious effort to develop a complete curriculum for which an interesting test would serve as an appropriate measure. Even in the test development process itself, serious homework can be skipped. A key step in the test development process is the drafting of a thoughtful statement of the specifications or blueprint for the test or test program. Such a specification statement is a kind of curricular document that not only guides test developers but also the users of the test program. Specification statements define basic concepts underlying the assessment, the outline of the contents, and the proportion of the assessment addressing each content category. Such statements can be omitted and replaced by a simple outline in a speeded-up test-development process. In the current debate on test-based reform, there is seldom if ever any mention of well-prepared specification statements.

Several years ago at ETS, when K-12 educators spoke glowingly of the teaching of critical thinking skills, albeit without clear definition, the prestigious Graduate Record Exam announced the addition of an analytical reasoning section to the existing GRE verbal and quantitative sections. In my personal search for a definition of critical thinking skills, I expected to find in the specifications for this new GRE offering a careful definition of analytical reasoning skills. I was shocked. There was no erudite specification statement or definition of analytical reasoning. It seems analytical reasoning skills in this case were simply the skills a person needed to do well on the kinds of puzzle-solving questions that were included in the section labeled "Analytical Reasoning." This section could just as well have been named "puzzle-solving." Here was a test with no curriculum even in sight, which was for a time accepted by America's graduate schools. It has now been discontinued after nearly a decade of use.

CURRICULUM ALIGNMENT

Test-based reformers do indeed recognize the existence of something called a curriculum. They call for "curriculum alignment." According to this notion, a curriculum that does not teach the contents of the test at the appropriate grade level is not aligned properly. The appropriate grade level is determined by the grade level of the test in which the content is tested. There is an important timing dimension in an aligned curriculum. One must teach the curricular subject matter in some proximity to when it is tested. In defense of this kind of alignment, one state superintendent argued there is a big difference between teaching to the test and teaching the test. In teaching to the test, if you are mirroring good teaching that will enhance learning, then, she asked, what is wrong with that? The only thing wrong with it is that it overrides the school's own curriculum; it interjects what might be new content based on a clever test question that does not really fit in the curriculum. The way to introduce new learning in the curriculum is to promote a thoughtful revision of the curriculum in the schools. This, however, is too slow for the instant "reforms" called for in this quick-fix era of test-based reform.

One benefit of test-based reforms is that they force the schools to look at their own day-to-day curriculum in terms of what is being taught and when. A school's own curriculum tends to be less visible because it is not the basis for any significant public reporting. In the information age, what is not publicly reported is not valued by the public. The answer, however, is not to align the curriculum to only those samples of learning that are publicly reported. The answer is to develop an information system that will enable schools to regularly report to their publics students' progress on the school's own curriculum. This would fill the void in which test-based reforms have propagated like weeds.

NOTES

1. Robert M. Gagne, "Curriculum Research and the Promotion of Learning," in *Perspectives of Curriculum Evaluation,* Chicago: Rand McNally, 1967, pp. 19ff.

2. Theodore R. Sizer, *Horace's Compromise: The Dilemma of the American High School,* Boston: Houghton Mifflin, 1984.

6

Hyping Student Performance Via the Cram Curriculum

External standardized testing in this era of test-based reform has become special event testing. Such testing includes both college admissions tests and state accountability tests. The dates for these tests are known well in advance, and intense efforts are focused on preparing students specifically for these special events. As pictures of student attainment, the tests are clearly posed portraits rather than random snapshots.

THE CRAM CURRICULUM

The process of intense preparation, using techniques refined in commercial test prep programs, might well be called the "cram curriculum." This cram curriculum can be delivered outside of school time by moonlighting teachers or by for-profit providers, who promise dramatic improvements in students' scores. The cram curriculum can also move into the school day and override the established curriculum of the schools. In a national survey of 1995–1996 SAT takers, more than 30 percent of high school students reported engaging in test-prep activities in their regular classes.[1] The principal features of the cram curriculum are:

- A total focus on knowledge and skill elements that are to be covered on the scheduled test, with no attention to other valuable aspects and applications of the subject matter.
- The timing of the instruction dictated by the schedule for testing without regard to the sequence being pursued in the curriculum.
- Concentration on the presentation of material only in the format in which it is covered on the test.

- An emphasis on developing test-wiseness so that knowledge of test development practices rivals in importance knowledge of the material tested.

An example of the last point is training students to avoid selecting the same answer on three consecutive questions. Supposedly, test developers always vary the correct answer option. The correct answer, for example, would never be "C" on three consecutive questions. With the disclosure of multiple-choice test forms following test disclosure legislation in 1980, this approach based on observed test development patterns and practices was featured in some coaching programs. One coaching school did a computer analysis of how test developers went about their business. Test developers then read this material and changed their practices.

DECEPTION: THE SHARED GOAL

The goal of students who cheat on tests is to make themselves look better than they really or typically are. The goal of the cram curriculum is exactly the same. It seeks to stage a hyped performance that over-represents what the student is typically able to do. John Hoven, an economist and activist parent, who challenged the test prep offerings of the Montgomery County (MD) public schools,[2] took the position that "Educators cheat to deceive parents and the business community about student achievement." Hoven added, "In this sense, all forms of teaching to the test are cheating (including) coaching during the exam, review sheets that reveal the test questions in advance, and the Superintendent's new test prep program." In this controversy, the test prep materials had students preparing for the test with questions in the same format as the test and with question content close to the actual content of the forthcoming test.

Professor Lorrie Shepard of the University of Colorado has frequently cautioned about the abuses of test prep or cram curriculum offerings.[3] She has noted that students can pretend to know more than they do on standardized tests "if we keep asking them to demonstrate skills in exactly the same format. As soon as you get kids comfortable with answering a question one way, you immediately ask it another way. They must get used to that flexible way of using a problem. If they only practice over and over again in formats that look just like the tests, it turns out they aren't very adept at anything but taking tests." This is where the cram curriculum differs from a bonafide curriculum. Both involve instruction. Nonetheless, they differ most clearly in their purpose and in their content.

As a parent, I have firsthand knowledge of excellent public schools that have a well-conceived and well-implemented curriculum. Nonetheless, I have been both amazed and discouraged at the extent that the cram curriculum has been interjected and allowed to override the regular program. At a recent parent night, an English teacher described how these cram elements were part of her assigned duties. She then quietly observed that she had her doubts about how appropriate it was to do any of this cramming business.

In the somewhat cynical climate associated with the cram curriculum and the dependence on external standardized testing, reports of actual cheating in the taking of the tests are not uncommon. This includes not only students who engage in copying and impersonations; it also includes active involvement in cheating by teachers and administrators. In an excellent school just down the road from where I live, the principal had to leave and a teacher was discharged for providing assistance to test-takers. Ironically, the staff at this top-flight public school felt under the gun to show improvement somehow. Kevin Bushweller in the *American School Board Journal* gave a rundown on other instances of cheating.[4]

- In West Virginia, a teacher received a letter of reprimand for helping students fix incorrect answers while they were taking a standardized test for accountability purposes. The teacher will be excused from proctoring tests for six years. Some parents are angry the teacher is still teaching.
- Several teachers in Maryland were temporarily suspended when it was discovered they had supplied some students with answers on the state's accountability assessment program.
- Kentucky has an external standardized testing program called the Kentucky Instructional Results Information System (KIRIS). The *Herald-Leader* newspaper reported that over several years the state had received 151 complaints that seemed to merit investigation of which 11 were investigated by the state.
- One school in Connecticut, ranking among the best schools in the state, saw its standing drop sharply when students were tested under controlled conditions. It seems that someone had for years been fixing up the answer sheets before returning them for scoring.

The same climate makes it difficult to discipline those involved; there is much pressure to look the other way.

External standardized testing has proven to be a kind of swamp and the breeding place for the cram curriculum and other, more direct forms of cheating. **Sadly, the most prominent result of test-based reform has been the alarming growth of the cram curriculum.** This growth has taken place both outside the schools and within the schools themselves. The test-prep industry has grown rapidly through the 1990s to become a two to three hundred million dollar industry, initially led by Stanley H. Kaplan's company, now a subsidiary of the Washington Post Company, and by the Princeton Review, a company that assails standardized testing while generating revenues in its more than 700 test-prep centers.

In addition, a host of small, often local, firms and consultants offer services in the test-prep arena that include offering assistance to the schools with the school's own cram curriculum. For students looking ahead to college admissions, many school systems offer their own after-school test-prep offerings at rates substantially below those of Kaplan and Princeton Review.

THE CRAM CURRICULUM AS THE CENTERPIECE IN SCHOOL REFORM

Unfortunately, the introduction and overwhelming growth of the cram curriculum has been the clearest major effect of educational reform effort at the turn of the century. This, in turn, is the inevitable result of using external, special-event standardized testing as the instructional information system that attempts to answer the accountability questions concerning U.S. schools.

It seems fair to expect educational reformers to have a "before picture" of what an unreformed school would look like and an "after picture" of what the school would look like after it was reformed. It is also fair to expect "reform" to be a term that bespeaks improvement. In the case of test-based reform, the school that has embraced this reform and with it the cram curriculum is certainly not an improved school.

The problem with the quick-fix, test-based reformers is their desire to tinker around the edges using external testing as a quick-fix information system rather than give serious attention to a school's primary curriculum and the kind of information system that will enable schools to report on this curriculum.

NOTES

1. Donald Powers and Donald Rock, "Effects of Coaching on SAT I: Reasoning Test Scores," *Journal of Educational Measurement,* Summer 1999, Vol. 36, No. 2, pp. 93–118.
2. Valerie Strauss, "Review Tests Go Too Far, Critics Say," *The Washington Post* 10 July 2001: A9.
3. Ibid.
4. Kevin Bushweller, "Teaching to the Test," *American School Board Journal* Vol. 184, No. 9, pp. 20–25, September 1997.

7

What Ever Happened to the Scholastic Aptitude Test?

In 1994, the College Board abandoned the original name of its flagship test for college admissions, the Scholastic Aptitude Test. They wanted to abandon the term "aptitude," apparently to quiet their critics, who were attacking from two directions. Some critics claimed the SAT measured intelligence and not mastery of school subjects. The coaching school people claimed it was not an aptitude test because they were able to coach or teach it to students with great success. They claimed to raise their clients' scores on average 120 points or more.[1]

For whatever the reason, the College Board in 1994 changed the name of the Scholastic Aptitude Test to the Scholastic Assessment Test. Shortly thereafter the Board abandoned this remarkable redundancy. They announced that what had been the Scholastic Assessment Test would simply be called SAT I. A companion series of tests, the College Board Achievement Tests covering various high school subjects, would be called SAT II. This was a sad decision in several ways.

First, the name change seemed to accept the vaunted claims of the test-prep industry that the SAT was very coachable and thus could be better described as an achievement test rather than an aptitude test. This was no service to education and testing, because the SAT was and remains an aptitude test. All SAT validity studies pertain to how well the SAT predicts student's success in their first year at college. The College Board has always described the SAT as a test of developed abilities.[2] It had always encouraged students to be serious in their studies in a college preparatory course of study as the most desirable way to prepare for the SAT. The College Board and most everyone else in testing had acknowledged for decades that there is overlap between the concepts of aptitude and achievement in testing.

THE OVERLAP BETWEEN APTITUDE AND ACHIEVEMENT

An achievement test assesses mastery of a specific subject or combination of subjects taught. The achievement test looks back to what the students were to have studied in their course of study. An aptitude test, on the other hand, assesses a set of teachable skills that predict future success. The aptitude test looks ahead to what the student will be asked to do in the future. The SAT was designed to predict academic success in the first year of college. Tests are classified by their intended use. The validity of a test always relates to how it is used.

A certain amount of untidiness flows from the overlap between aptitude and achievement assessments. A clue to the difficulty comes when one looks at a specific test question and tries to identify it as either an aptitude or an achievement test item. It might well be both. All achievement tests also measure aptitude to some degree. Students who did well on the Biology I test are likely to do well on the Biology II. The best single predictor of freshman college grades are high school grade point averages, which are used in the college admissions process, in effect, as an aptitude measure. Now, no one would ever suggest that high school grades were measures of aptitude; they are clearly measures of achievement.

The ACT is a college admissions test taken by over 1.1 million students in 2001. In contrast to the SAT, the ACT has always claimed to be an achievement test broadly reflecting what is taught in high schools. In the admissions process, however, the ACT is used just like the SAT to predict aptitude for college work. Achievement and aptitude are constructs that do indeed overlap. On the achievement/aptitude continuum, tests can be located at different points. The ACT is closer to the achievement end than the SAT (now SAT I), which is closer to the aptitude end of the continuum.

All aptitude tests assess achievement; they measure developed abilities. In a basic 1995 work entitled *School Testing: What Parents and Educators Need to Know*, Professor Estelle Gellman of Hofstra University[3] describes and explains the wide array of tests used in schools. Professor Gellman insists that even the school-administered tests that are labeled IQ tests should be considered and interpreted as "scholastic aptitude tests," because they measure developed abilities. These aptitude tests cover a range of knowledge skills that is much broader and less specific than the knowledge and skills covered in (say) a Biology I test.

Because both aptitude and achievement tests cover developed skills and knowledge, they are both coachable (i.e., affected by short-term instruction) but to a far different degree. Achievement tests are extremely coachable. An intensive review before a final exam does wonders! Aptitude tests are likewise coachable but only slightly.

COACHING SCHOOL CLAIMS

A regrettable note in the SAT name change is the implication that the College Board appeared to accept the exaggerated claims of success advertised by two largest coaching schools, Stanley Kaplan and Princeton Review, which both maintain that the SAT is extremely coachable. The two coaching schools claim average gains of 120 to 140 points based on their own surveys.

In considering score gains, it is important to pay attention to the maturation effect on SAT scores. Students tend to do better after another year of schooling. The score gain from one test date to another has to take into account this typical maturation before this gain can be attributed to coaching.

In 1995–1996, ETS researchers Donald Powers and Donald Rock[4] conducted a survey study of some 6,700 randomly selected SAT test-takers on the effects of coaching by Kaplan or Princeton Review, the results showed an average score gain of 8 points for the verbal scores and 18 points for the math. In this study, score gain was determined by the difference in scores between coached and uncoached students. Neither group was entirely without something akin to coaching. The coached students, those taking either of the two commercial test prep courses, also took other test prep steps in their free time, as did the uncoached students. Over half of both groups read the basic material ("Taking the SAT") and took a practice test. Over a third of both groups had some of their regular class time devoted to test prep activities, which is further evidence of the intrusiveness of the cram curriculum. As shown in this survey, coached students who took the commercial test prep courses were more likely to be from a more well-to-do family and viewed their previous test scores as under-representing their abilities.

The Powers and Rock study was similar to a host of other studies published in scholarly journals. In a 1990 meta-analysis that looked at 48 separate studies, Becker concluded that coaching increased the average SAT verbal scores by 9 points and the math scores by 19 points.[5] These kinds of numbers support the use of the term "scholastic aptitude test" to describe the SAT.

WHAT GOOD WAS IT?

Ironically, in February 2001, several years after the name change, Richard Atkinson, the president of the University of California,[6] asked the university's academic senate to discard the renamed SAT I because it was a measure of student aptitude. He favored increased reliance on the SAT II, the achievement tests. Subsequently, researchers at UC found that the SAT II achievement tests were better than the SAT I at predicting freshman-year grades for UC students.[7] Atkinson was certainly right to identify the renamed SAT I as an aptitude measure.

In the revision that accompanied the name change, one major change, rather publicly considered, was the introduction of a writing sample in the SAT I. This was dropped, however, partly as a result of the strong objections of Asian-American educators in California, who thought this addition would handicap Asian-American students. They presumed the Asian- American students would do better in the multiple-choice format than in actual writing. By coincidence, several weeks later, for a presentation at a conference, I obtained new information from Advanced Placement testing, which for each subject used both multiple-choice and open-ended or written exams. On every exam, Asian Americans did better on the open-ended or writing exercise than on the multiple-choice section. In comparison to other groupings of students, they did quite well on both sections.

In my work at ETS, I was occasionally asked about coaching schools. My own position was resource based. For students with the time and the money readily at hand, I suggested they go for it. For students for whom either time or money was in short supply, I counseled caution. I strongly supported the early position statements of the College Board that identified serious pursuit of the school's own college prep curriculum as the best preparation for the SAT.

What the Board wanted in those days was to have students pursuing only one curriculum, the one their school offered. At all costs, what they wanted to avoid was having the students' attention divided between two courses of study, a school course of study and an SAT-prep course of study. Like it not, that is where high schools are now. The renaming of the SAT signaled the victory of the cram curriculum.

With the name change came increased efforts by the College Board to market its own test prep materials and services. All in all, not a happy chapter!

NOTES

1. Donald Powers and Donald Rock, "Effects of Coaching on SAT I: Reasoning Test Scores," *Journal of Educational Measurement,* Summer 1999, Vol. 36, No. 2, pp. 93–118.
2. An early College Board/ETS internal document called the "Green Book" (this work is no longer available).
3. Estelle S. Gellman, *"School Testing: What Parents and Educators Need to Know,"* Westport, Conn.: Praeger, 1995, pp. 70–71.
4. Powers and Rock, op cit.
5. Ibid., p. 113.
6. John Gehring, "UC President Pitches Plan to End Use of SAT in Admissions," *Education Week,* 28 February 2001.
7. Tom Kim, "SAT II Better Predictor of College Success, UC Says," *Education Week,* 7 November 2001.

8

Avoiding the Information Age: The Road Not Considered

The principal reason that external standardized testing and the cram curriculum have taken such a dominant place in American schools is educators have largely avoided the Information Age and the amazing possibilities it offers.

When microcomputers arrived at the classroom doors throughout the country, educators faced what amounted to a fork in the road. Computers could go on the teacher's desk in the front of the room or in the back of the room for student use. They also could have gone in both places. Instead, they were placed in the back of the classroom, in media centers, or in computer labs. The option of placing computers on teachers' desks with the idea of linking them and the other school staff together in an instructional management information system was not seriously considered, as it seems. At this fork, the road represented by "teacher use" was not only "the road less traveled," it was "the road never even seriously considered."

Outside education, the predominant use of microcomputing technology has been as a powerful information tool, usually used in some networked configuration. For example, banks, long seen as bastions of conservatism, have exploited this new technology to create a nationwide system of ATMs. Most businesses use spreadsheet, accounting, and database software. Managers everywhere now have access to powerful tools to better manage their enterprises.

The Information Age has helped managers almost everywhere, but it has not reached instructional managers in schools. In fact, even the term "instructional management" seems to have been preempted by those working in the field of distance learning. School principals, the people officially responsible for instruction, often know more about what goes on in the hallways and the parking lot than in the classrooms. What teachers are actually teaching and what students are actually learning in classrooms, daily or weekly, are not reported anywhere. The only reporting done after two to three months takes the form of grades, which reflect primarily a teacher's unstated assumptions about what constitutes "A" or "B" or "C" work. Grades stand alone without any data as to their possible significance and validity. This is the Information Age void that external standardized tests are used to fill. No wonder!

THE CHOSEN ROAD: COMPUTERS FOR STUDENT USE

The failure to consider the use of computers by teachers in an instructional information system might have been understandable had the students' use of computers in the back of the classrooms proven to be a huge success. The prospect of such success did receive some press. Education writer Jay Matthews[1] pointed out that Al Gore, as a congressman and "young seer of the new age," saw the potential for computers to improve education as "more dramatic than any invention since writing." Others predicted that computers would change the very nature of the educational process.

Student use of computers in the classroom, however, has not been successful enough to dazzle or distract educators from considering other possibilities. Classroom use has been held back by several factors including:

- the lack of computers (only two to three) per classroom resulting in classroom management problems
- a poor fit between computer offerings and the course of study
- the comparative differences in familiarity with computers that favor the students over the teachers.

The research on the level of computer use up to the year 2001 has not been especially encouraging. As William Bennett summarized the picture, "The vast majority of teachers have not begun to integrate computers into their teaching. Computers often sit in classrooms unused or used for activities having no real impact on learning or academic success. Students sit at terminals with little or no instruction and very few quality programs to help them along."[2] Bennett cited an ETS study that found students who used computers once a week did less well on national tests than did those who used computers less frequently. Home use of computers by eighth graders did correlate with achievement, while home use by fourth graders correlated negatively with achievement. This latter group may have concentrated on gaming.

Computers have not reduced the achievement disparity between educational haves and have-nots. After years of federal and state programs funding public school technology, low-income and minority fourth-graders spend more time at computers than their peers, but that additional time has been associated with an even wider gap in educational achievement. Student growth in achievement most directly results from focusing on the learning task. If the computer distracts rather than focuses students' attention on the learning task, the effect could indeed be negative.

Clearly, the road that was chosen did not lead to the kinds of success that would hold the undivided attention of educators and prevent consideration of other uses of the computer in schools.

ARE EDUCATORS "DATA AVERSE"?

Being "data averse" could be defined as having a penchant for avoiding the creation of publicly interpretable, quantitative information. Educators seemed to have this penchant. To call this a conspiracy of silence would be a reach. It is difficult to allege a conspiracy, for the reason that no one ever talks about the subject. There has been no open debate on whether or not schools need more quantitative data in a comprehensive instructional information system. It seems never to have been considered.

For years, the accepted wisdom in the management of schools is that publicly interpretable data are a potential source of trouble. This accepted wisdom greeted the Information Age as a development that should be praised and then avoided. A publication of the Knight Higher Education Collaborative[3] did address the question of the use of data in higher education management. The discussion focused on the use of information in an early-warning system, where "leaders with access to information were expected to act." The authors then noted: "Nothing can be less productive than having alarms sounded in the media and other public venues on the basis of numbers intended as early-warning beacons for institutional leaders." School managers must be in a position to monitor their programs and have time to address numbers that serve as early warnings. Presumably, this kind of thinking underlies the accepted wisdom in K–12 education that data spell trouble. This needs to be addressed. In any information system, careful attention must be given to which numbers are for early warning purposes and which are for public accountability. This must be sorted out so that the information system can serve both purposes.

SIGNS OF BEGINNINGS: DATA WAREHOUSING

In 1996, IBM funded the Broward County Public Schools with a "Reinventing Education" grant of in-kind services worth $2 million for implementing a data warehouse. A data warehouse has been defined as a repository of information that imports, standardizes, and integrates data from a school district's various operational systems, databases and different computer networks used for day-to day operations and state and federal reports. These databases include enrollment, attendance, testing, medical records, grades, demographics, and participation in ESL, school lunch, Advanced Placement or other kinds of programs.

One author has described school systems as data-rich but knowledge-poor.[4] Data warehousing addresses this condition by making all the school district's different databases relational. This early Florida venture showed that teachers were ready for more information and eager to develop their data analysis skills. They also became more involved in assuring the quality of the data they put into the system. In one school, teachers looked at reading scores and math placements and found several students in advanced algebra with very low reading scores. Their reading problems had heretofore been overlooked. This was a start toward harnessing the power of the information age.

In 1999, as he was beginning to offer a new information management and data-warehousing system called Learning Landscape, Philip Streifer saw the schools "as awash in data" and their leaders as "unable to analyze the volumes of data because the technology programs to do so are either unavailable or too expensive."[5] According to Streifer, a professor at the University of Connecticut, "unfortunately the technological revolution transforming the world of business, medicine, and manufacturing is largely unavailable to educators."

At this same time, in a work called *Raising the Standard,* Denis Doyle and Susan Pimental offered an eight-step reform program, which included as one step the conduct of an "academic analysis."[6] An academic analysis "quantifies, measures, and relates the three major dimensions of the school process, resources, context, and results." These authors contend that "analyzing the academic performance of American schools is almost unprecedented, so pressure for it is lacking." They, however, see this pressure now coming from the demands for accountability. They equate this academic analysis to what is described in business as "bench-marking." They also call for the creation of a data warehouse as an essential step. They detail what they see in the warehouse and the multi-dimensional questions they would formulate to query the database in what they call a school management information system.

These are the early rays of the dawn of the Information Age in American schools.

NOTES

1. Jay Matthews, "In The Beginning," *The Washington Post Magazine,* 16 September 2001: 15.
2. William J. Bennett, "The Next Chapter in American Education," *Hoover Digest* 2001 No. 1, www-hoover.Stanford.edu/publications/digest/011/Bennett. html
3. "The Data Made Me Do It," Policy Perspectives, the Knight Higher Education Collaborative, March 2000, Vol. 9, No. 2.
4. Lars Kongshem, "Smart Data, Mining the School District Warehouse," *Electronic School,* September 1999, p. 14 (A Supplement to the *American School Board Journal,* vol. 186, no. 9).
5. Philip Streifer, "Putting the 'Byte' in Educational Decision-making" *Education Week,* 17 March 1999.
6. Denis P. Doyle and Susan Pimentel, *Raising the Standard,* Thousand Oaks, Calif.: Corwin Press, 1998, pp. 48–72.

9

National Attention to Content and Performance Standards

The most promising element in the accountability and reform movement is the attention and importance given to content and performance standards. This movement advocates "standards-based education," which requires students to be instructed and assessed in reference to prescribed levels of performance on certain tasks. The movement, while it creates a positive focus on student attainment and carefully defined goals, could be translated into lasting reforms or prove to be another in a long history of fads. To succeed, it must include the incorporation of these standards into an information system that is the centerpiece of the day-to-day workings of the schools.

WHAT DO STANDARDS LOOK LIKE?

The Council for Basic Education (CBE) has served this movement toward standards-based education by compiling materials to educate all interested parties on what content and performance standards are and how they are to be used.[1] The Council offers the following definitions:

- **Content standards:** Statements that define expectations for students in terms of knowledge and skills.
- **Curriculum:** The description of how and what students will be taught in the relevant course(s) to achieve the objectives described in the content standards.
- **Performance standards:** Descriptions of the kind of mastery students are supposed to achieve, normally given in connection with a content standard. Content standards identify something to be learned;

performance standards identify how well students are supposed to learn it. Performance standards sometimes identify more than one level of achievement for a content standard, and label each level accordingly (for example, basic, proficient, advanced.)

The term "benchmarking" is also used in reference to standards. Some benchmarking is related to grade levels and some to what students in other countries attained on international assessments in math and science. These benchmarks indicate what students are expected to do at a certain point in their schooling.

EXAMPLES OF CONTENT STANDARDS

To illustrate the idea of content standards, sample content standards in language arts, math, and science are presented here. Presented in Figure 9.1 are slightly modified excerpts from the New Jersey Core Curriculum Content Standards.

For each content standard, appropriate performance standards would need to be formulated for assessing mastery at the basic, proficient, and advanced levels. These would describe what students at each of the levels could do in reference to the grade-level benchmarks. Additional benchmarks would need to be elaborated to describe the elements to be mastered in the years leading up to grades four, eight, and twelve.

STANDARDS AT THE CROSSROADS

Most all schools or school districts have content standards in one format or another that are the basis for the school's academic program. The extent to which these schemata are used and kept up-to-date may vary greatly. In 1998, Christopher Cross of the Council for Basic Education saw "the push for academic content and performance standards" as "the most important and enduring change to impact schools."[2] At the same time, he acknowledged being asked often "in forums across the country whether standards are here to stay or simply a passing fad that will soon be replaced by another fad."

This same year, the Thomas Fordham Foundation published a report on the "State of State Standards," which assigned low marks to most state standards.[3] The authors stressed the importance of treating academic-content

Figure 9.1

Language Arts Standard 3.3:
All Students Will Write In Clear, Concise, Organized Language That Varies In Content And Form For Different Audiences And Purposes.

Descriptive Statement: Writing is a complex process that may be used for self or others in communication, expression, and learning. Proficient writers have a repertoire of strategies that enables them to vary forms, style, and conventions in order to write for different audiences, contexts, and purposes. Students should be taught strategies that will assist them in writing clearly and in crafting their texts with appropriate conventions of spelling, grammar, and punctuation as they revise, edit, and publish. They should learn to examine their writing not only as a product but also as a mode of thinking.

Grade Level Benchmarks

By the end of Grade 4, students:

1. Use speaking, listening, reading, and viewing to assist with writing.

2. Write from experiences, thoughts, and feelings.

3. Use writing to extend experience.

4. Write for a variety of purposes, such as to persuade, enjoy, entertain, learn, inform, record, respond to reading, and solve problems.

5. Write on self-selected topics in a variety of literary forms.

6. Write collaboratively and independently.

7. Use a variety of strategies and activities, such as brainstorming, listing, discussion, drawing, role playing, note-taking, and journal writing, for finding and developing ideas about which to write.

8. Write to synthesize information from multiple sources.

9. Use figurative language, such as simile, metaphor, and analogies to expand meaning.

10. Revise content, organization and other aspects of writing, using self, peer, and teacher collaborative feedback (the shared responses of others).

11. Edit writing for developmentally appropriate syntax, spelling, grammar, usage, and punctuation.

12. Publish writing in a variety of formats.

13. Establish and use criteria for self and group evaluation of written products.

Figure 9.1 continued

14. Develop a portfolio or collection of writings.

Building upon knowledge and skills gained in the preceding grades, by the end of Grade 8, students:

    15. Understand that written communication can affect the behavior of others.

    16. Write technical materials, such as instructions for playing a game, that include specific details.

    17. Cite sources of information.

Building upon knowledge and skills gained in the preceding grades, by the end of Grade 12, students:

    18. Write for real audiences and purposes, such as job applications, business letters, college applications, and memoranda.

    19. Write a research paper that synthesizes and cites data.

Mathematics Standard 4.7:
All Students Will Develop Spatial Sense And An Ability To Use Geometric Properties And Relationships To Solve Problems In Mathematics And In Everyday Life

Descriptive Statement: Spatial sense is an intuitive feel for shape and space. It involves the concepts of traditional geometry, including an ability to recognize, visualize, represent, and transform geometric shapes. It also involves other, less formal ways of looking at two- and three-dimensional space, such as paper-folding, transformations, tessellations, and projections.

Grade Level Benchmarks

By the end of Grade 4, students:

    1. Recognize spatial relationships such as the direction, orientation, and perspectives of objects in space, their relative shapes and sizes, and the relations between objects and their shadows or projections.

    2. Recognize relationships among shapes, such as congruence, symmetry, similarity, and self-similarity.

    3. Recognize properties of three- and two-dimensional shapes using concrete objects, drawings, and computer graphics.

    4. Use properties of three- and two-dimensional shapes to identify, classify, and describe shapes.

    5. Investigate and predict the results of combining, subdividing, and changing shapes.

Figure 9.1 continued

6. Use tessellations to explore properties of geometric shapes and their relationships to the concepts of area and perimeter.

7. Recognize geometric transformations such as rotations (turns), reflections (flips), and translations (slides).

8. Develop the concepts of coordinates and paths, using maps, tables, and grids.

9. Understand the variety of ways in which geometric shapes and objects can be measured.

10. Investigate the occurrence of geometry in nature, art, and other areas.

Building upon knowledge and skills gained in the preceding grades, by the end of Grade 8, students:

11. Relate two-dimensional and three-dimensional geometry using shadows, perspectives, projections and maps.

12. Understand and apply the concepts of symmetry, similarity and congruence.

13. Identify, describe, compare, and classify plane and solid geometric figures.

14. Understand the properties of lines and planes, including parallel and perpendicular lines and planes, and intersecting lines and planes and their angles of incidence.

15. Recognize the relationships among geometric transformations (translations, reflections, rotations, and dilations), tessellations (tilings), and congruence and similarity.

16. Develop, understand, and apply a variety of strategies for determining perimeter, area, surface area, angle measure, and volume.

17. Understand and apply the Pythagorean Theorem.

18. Recognize patterns produced by processes of geometric change, relating iteration, approximation, and fractals.

19. Investigate, explore, and describe geometry in nature and real-world applications, using models, manipulatives, and appropriate technology.

Building upon knowledge and skills gained in the preceding grades, and demonstrating continued progress in Indicators 16 and 19 above, by the end of Grade 12, students:

20. Understand and apply properties involving angles, parallel lines, and perpendicular lines.

Figure 9.1 continued

21. Analyze properties of three-dimensional shapes by constructing models and by drawing and interpreting two-dimensional representations of them.

22. Use transformations, coordinates, and vectors to solve problems in Euclidean geometry.

23. Use basic trigonometric ratios to solve problems involving indirect measurement.

24. Solve real-world and mathematical problems using geometric models.

25. Use inductive and deductive reasoning to solve problems and to present reasonable explanations of and justifications for the solutions.

26. Analyze patterns produced by processes of geometric change, and express them in terms of iteration, approximation, limits, self-similarity, and fractals.

27. Explore applications of other geometries in real-world contexts.

Science Standard 5.1:
All Students Will Learn To Identify Systems Of Interacting Components And Understand How Their Interactions Combine To Produce The Overall Behavior Of The System

Descriptive Statement: The natural world and the world built by humans both provide examples of systems where interacting parts work together as a whole. This standard asks students to analyze, understand, and design systems of integrating parts.

Grade Level Benchmarks

By the end of Grade 4, students:

1. Recognize that most things are made of components that, when assembled, can do things they could not do separately.

2. Recognize that since the components of a system usually influence one another, a system may not work if a component is missing.

3. Diagram the components of a system.

Building upon knowledge and skills gained in the preceding grades, by the end of Grade 8, students:

4. Describe components of a system and how they influence one another.

5. Recognize that most systems are components of larger systems and that the output of one component can become the input to other components.

Figure 9.1 continued

6. Disassemble and reassemble the components of a system, analyzing how they interact with each other.

Building upon knowledge and skills gained in the preceding grades, by the end of Grade 12, students:

7. Recognize that the behavior of a system may be different from the behavior of its components.

8. Explain how feedback can be used to control the behavior of a system.

9. Identify and diagram feedback loops that occur in biological or ecological systems.

10. Identify and diagram feedback loops designed for common control systems, such as home light switches and thermostats.

standards as the starting point in the creation of a complete accountability system. Chester Finn, one of the authors, commented, "We do worry a bit that states are going to tend to treat good content standards as the end of the matter; it's like having a fine recipe in the cookbook but not actually cooking."

To pursue Finn's cookbook analogy, the states can provide schools and districts with the classic recipe in the form of well-defined content standards. The cooking, however, is done at the school level where the recipe is adapted to local tastes. Each district or school must, in the final analysis, have its own academic content standards. These content standards need to be incorporated as the basic schema or framework in a computer-based instructional management information system. Every teacher would use this system to identify the content standards and performance standards she or he is working on with each class group. Teachers would also use the system with these same standards for reporting on student progress based on teacher observational ratings that draw on a host of assessment forms. With such a system, the cooking will really begin. Fortunately, the information age has presented educators with the way to move these content and performance standards documents off the proverbial shelf and into an operational system for day-to-day school management.

The whole standards movement could easily prove to be another passing educational fad, if standards are not incorporated into a classroom-connected instructional management information system resident in the computer on each teacher's desk. Building the standards into the day-to-day operations of the schools will also force standards to undergo a reality-check. University of Washington Professor Paul Hill saw state standards as lacking an empirical basis. According to Hill,[4] "Standards have been developed as airy visions that satisfy all factions of the professional education community. Enthusiasts for different subjects . . . have all found a secure place for themselves. . . . Business leaders are discovering that the groups that developed state standards were never asked whether they could prepare most or all students to meet the standards."

The standards that are incorporated in a school's instructional management information system must pass a careful reality check. This use of standards as the focus of an individual school's program would prevent the standards movement, in Hill's words, from being seen "as yet another loosely defined effort to stir up commitment and exhort teachers to higher performance."

In an April 2001 article entitled "A Critical Fork in the Road," Tony Wagner and Tom Vander Ark saw many states facing a critical choice between focusing schools on "passing the test," or focusing on meaningful student learning.[5] They point out that "states that have become too dependent on high stakes, high standards tests" have another option: build an accountability system that helps students focus on producing quality work. This latter option would feature what they call "robust public information systems" that "would allow states more freedom to license alternative systems of standards and assessments to networks of schools," rather than to impose a single arbitrary definition of "high standards." The core of any such accountability system that focuses on quality student work and information systems requires the incorporation of the local school's content and performance standards into a computer-based instructional information system used each daily by every teacher.

COMPUTER-BASED OBSERVATIONAL RATINGS

Earlier I mentioned a computer-based observational rating system that a clerk used to describe the leased car I was about to return. His technology was in stark contrast to my experience at a national education conference where a "new" primary reading record was the featured attraction. Because the room was filled to overflowing, I stood in the doorway long enough to see the shape of this "exciting" new assessment tool. The new record was a series of open-ended questions to which the teacher would respond by writing brief paragraphs. While for many, it had the merit of not being a standardized test, it struck me that here was an assessment tool that could have been introduced a century before. With considerable writing required from teachers, I wondered how many teachers would soon grow weary and give up.

Had this same tool been introduced in a computer-based format, teachers, parents, students, and instructional managers all would have been better off. The most likely possible responses to each question could be easily identified in advance by a team of experienced teachers. These would be displayed on a pull-down screen as options for the teachers, always with an open option called "other-please specify," for unanticipated responses. Another pull-down screen for each response option would present a number of descriptors for the teachers to select. Again, the "other-please specify" option would be available. In such a report, the teacher could quickly and accurately describe the strengths and weakness of individual students and of the class as a group. This information would have several uses. In different forms, it could serve principals, teachers, parents, students, and instructional managers, who would all be in a position to see a group-profile of the readers by classroom and grade level and to identify common difficulties. The thinking of experienced teachers and reading specialists would be "built into this system," in order to benefit every teacher, especially the beginning teacher.

Such a computer-supported system is needed to save the standards movement from ending up as another passing fad.

NOTES

1. *Standards for Excellence in Education,* Washington, D.C.: Council for Education, 1998.
2. Christopher Cross, "The Standards Wars: Some Lessons Learned" *Education Week,* 21 October 1998.
3. Kathleen Kennedy Manzo, "Many States Add Up to 'D' in Review," *Education Week,* 8 July 1998.
4. Paul T. Hill "Getting Standards Right," *The Weekly Standard,* 10 December 2001, Vol. 7, No. 13, (rear cover compliments of the Hoover Institution).
5. Tony Wagner and Tom Vander Ark, "A Critical Fork in the Road," *Education Week,* 11 April 2001.

10

Teacher Knows Best: Standardizing Teacher Judgment

In September 2001, the Cleveland Public Schools began to introduce more descriptive report cards that reported what students can and cannot do.[1] They began with math. There is a check-off on eleven math skills at grade two, such as "identifies two- and three- dimensional shapes" and "learns about chance and probability." The district's executive director of research, evaluation, and testing, Peter Robinson, commented that once the grading system improves the description of student progress, it will be a more telling indicator than proficiency test scores. He added, "Student work in the classroom is much richer in terms of describing what they can and cannot do." The Cleveland staff has recognized what should be common knowledge: the teacher knows best. Cleveland is going to work on a system that enables teachers systematically to share what they know.

THE INVESTMENT IN TEACHER KNOWLEDGE

Schools and school systems spend millions of dollars for teachers' salaries and inservice training to enable them to learn what their students can and cannot do. This is always the largest single school-budget item or, if you will, the largest single investment the school makes. In terms of its information value, it has been an almost entirely neglected investment. Teacher judgment is by far the most important information asset that the schools have created—and one that is subsequently seldom used.

As a parent, I have felt confident that the teacher could tell me what my youngster could or could not do in the subjects taught by that teacher. As a rule, teachers know their students and the quality of their work in the subjects or skills they are teaching them. They see the students

57

responding to questions in class, completing homework assignments, taking quizzes, doing projects, etc. Teachers have the answers to the accountability questions.

At the outset, any systematic use of teacher judgment must begin on the basis of a presumption of confidence in their judgments. This is what is called "face validity." A measure has "face validity," when it certainly looks like it should be valid. Face validity must be the starting point in the absence of research or validating evidence on the accuracy of teacher judgments.

Research documenting the validity of teacher judgment is, at present, shamefully hard to come by. About ten years ago, I read a brief monograph summarizing a few scattered studies that affirmed the validity of teacher judgment. The federally funded, master file on educational research called ERIC lists over 10,000 descriptors available for searching this comprehensive educational research database. As of 2001, "teacher judgment" did not even make list. The extent to which this obvious information asset is overlooked is one of the most appalling phenomena in education today.

The one piece of research that obliquely affirms teacher judgment deals with the predictability of high school grades relative to success in the first year of college. High school grade point averages have continually shown up as the best single predictor of success in college. College admissions tests have come in a close second. The argument for using these tests is that, when combined with high school grades, they enhance the predictability information that admissions people are seeking.

STANDARDIZING TEACHER JUDGMENT

The two educational assessment approaches that have received the widest acclaim in recent years have been portfolios and Advanced Placement testing. They have one important element in common: both require and depend upon the standardization of teacher judgment. The key element in portfolio assessments is the development of scoring rubrics and work samples that document the quality of student work expected at each score point. (Rubrics are discussed in chapter 14.) With such guides, the scores assigned by teacher to student work samples become "standardized" and thus publicly interpretable. This same kind of standardization of judgment is essential in the scoring of writing exercises in testing programs.

In the scoring of the open-ended or essay portion of the Advanced Placement Tests, ETS has worked with the training of scorers to the point that only one scorer reads each paper and assigns it a score. This score becomes a part of what will become a standardized score of 1 to 5 that college staff can interpret and use in their admissions process and possibly for the awarding of college credit.

The work that remains for Cleveland's Peter Robinson is to help his Cleveland colleagues make what are, in effect, standardized ratings on their report cards. That the Cleveland staff began with math in the lower grades was to be expected. Everyone always begin with math in any process involving standards and assessment. Math has clearly defined content and progressions. The more difficult work lies ahead.

ENVISIONING AN INFORMATION SYSTEM APPROACH

Using a computer-based information system promises to be the most effective way to make teacher judgments standardized and publicly interpretable. Here is how such an approach would work.

The school's academic content and performance standards would be elaborated to cover all the grade levels in the school to provide the structure or "bones" for such a system. For each content standard, a full array of performance standards would be described at three levels, basic, proficient, and advanced. For each performance standard at each level, the expected level of mastery would be carefully described with concrete examples and scoring rubrics. This would put at each teacher's fingertips an awesome amount of shared expertise.

As they approached the beginning of a semester with a new class roster in hand, teachers would access from the data warehouse a group profile of the class they were about to teach. This profile would come from combining data from the scheduling computer program and the instructional information computer program. This profile would tell the teachers where their students were in terms of mastery of the content and performance standards the teacher was expecting to address. Teachers could then select which of the standards they chose to address in the coming semester.

Much expertise would be built into this "smart system." Every teacher would have instant access to explanations of each academic content standard and set of performance standards. With each content standard and accompanying performance standards, the teacher would have a number of prompts and help screens. Pull down screens would offer possible descriptors for describing levels of performance. Samples of quality work at various level of performance would be instantly available. At every step, the information system would enable the teacher to be confident in making a clear judgment in terms that are understood by all users of the system.

A system of this type would enable teachers to make standardized judgments that would create a powerful and comprehensive array of information on what is being taught and what is being learned. These new data would be, in Peter Robinson's words, "more telling" than any proficiency tests. (The proficiency tests, however, would not disappear; they would serve an important but less central role, as one among several validity checks on the new data.)

In the language of business information systems, the most basic component of the system is the transaction processing system that keeps track of the company's transactions (sales, units manufactured, deliveries and pick-ups, etc.).[2] An information system that tracked teaching and learning in every classroom as reported in standardized teacher judgments would capture the transactional level in schools. This kind of instructional information system would be the answer to the demands of accountability. Instructional managers, school administrators, parents, students, and interested publics would know in real time (not a year or so later) what students are learning and what they are able to do.

NOTES

1. Angela Townsend and Janet Okoben, "Cleveland District Testing More Detailed Report Cards," *The Plain Dealer,* 25 September 2001.

2. Kenneth Laudon and Jane Price Laudon, *Essentials of Management Information Systems,* Upper Saddle River, N. J.: Prentice Hall, 1997, pp. 33–36.

11

Envisioning an Instructional Management Information System

The Information Age brings to the schoolhouse all the tools needed for implementing an instructional management information system and ending the overreliance on external standardized testing. Such an information system would focus on a school's own curriculum and enable the local school to provide far richer accountability information.

Such an information system would need to have three components:

- data warehousing, which would combine the school and school district's various, already existing computer-based systems into one "warehouse" or relational database
- the school's academic content and performance standards elaborated to serve every grade level and entered into a computer-based format, providing the structure for the accountability system, and
- Software tools that enable teachers, using handheld or desktop computers to make clear and publicly understandable judgments in reporting student progress toward the standards set by the school.

The information system described here would not eliminate the need for external and internal standardized, multiple-choice testing. With its natural efficiencies, such testing would serve effectively as a validation tool to monitor the workings of the school's information systems. Such use would, however, eliminate the need for special-event prepping and the cram curriculum.

DATA WAREHOUSING: RESCUING THE DATA-RICH BUT KNOWLEDGE-POOR

As explained earlier, data warehousing overcomes the condition faced by many districts that are data-rich and knowledge-poor, because the districts cannot relate one set of information in one system to another database housed in a different system. In how many schools do teachers, as they begin the school year with a new class, have a profile of the prior academic performance of the new class? Such information would require the scheduling software to relate to the academic information database. A simple matter for the data warehouse!

The computer systems or programs coming together in one warehouse might include the following kinds of information:

- attendance records
- scheduling
- health records
- deportment records
- family background information
- participation in special programs such as English as a Second Language, Title I, school lunch, etc.
- participation in extracurricular programs
- academic information such as grades and placement in special programs such as Advanced Placement
- external test scores such as state, country, or district-wide tests, college admissions tests, and the Armed Services Vocational Aptitude Battery (ASVAB)
- school-administered vocational guidance inventories
- school-administered inventories on learning styles, etc.

Not all of these files would be available to all school personnel. Provisions would need to be made to protect confidentiality, e.g., with medical and family background information.

Using more primitive tools, I worked for a school district where I examined data they had on hand. Putting together high school grades and student performance on the College Board's Achievement Tests showed that math grading was more rigorous than grading in other subjects. Students getting "C's" were among the tops in the country. Relations of this type could be routinely monitored with a data warehouse.

In another district where I worked, it turned out that the small number of seniors who had not passed the school's basic skills test required for graduation were the same students who were most often absent. They did not come to school often enough to even take the test.

Data warehousing is an essential first step in creating an accountability system that will give the kinds of complete answers people demand.

REPORTING AT THE TRANSACTIONAL LEVEL

The other two components of the proposed information system deal with generating and reporting interpretable or "standardized" information from within the classroom. This system begins with a computer on every teacher's desk.

The assumption here is that the academic content standards that a school or school district has adopted are its central focus. That is what these schools are about! While these standards do not cover all the content that a teacher may choose to teach in his or her class, the standards do cover the academic content, divided across grades and subjects that every teacher must address. If these standards are to have the impact desired, they must be incorporated in an operational information system that is used for reporting what teachers are teaching and what students are learning. The standards must provide the "bones" of the accountability system.

Academic content standards, first of all, need to be elaborated, so that they are benchmarked for every grade level. Performance standards for each of the content standards need also to be developed and incorporated into the system. These performance standards translate the academic content standards and benchmarks into descriptions and samples of student work or performances that teachers can observe and clearly rate. At this point, the experience and expertise of a team of very able teachers in each subject area must be incorporated into the computer-based system. These teachers are the ones who, behind the scenes, translate the standards into observable realities. For example, in reference to a science content standard on identifying and understanding the interacting components of a system, a performance standard might require students to diagram the components of a system. For this standard, the expert teachers would include in the information system descriptions and samples of such diagrams at the basic, proficient, and advanced levels.

A parallel for the process exists in the grading of written work by persons not directly familiar with the student who produced the work. The key step in conducting a successful scoring of student written exercises is the behind-the-scenes selection of "training papers" by the lead-teacher or expert, who identifies "training" or sample papers that demonstrate what is excellent (4), good (3), fair (2), and poor (1). The expert can also describe why these papers are excellent, good, etc. This process makes possible the standardization of hundreds of judgments made by teachers. Before teachers begin to rate essay papers, they practice with these training papers until they see (and routinely rate) "four-level" papers as "four-level papers" and "three-level papers" as "three-level papers," and so on. With such tools, teachers can internalize standards and apply them consistently. In essence, this is what it means to "standardize" teacher judgments.

The work of scoring writing exercises or other work samples in a standardized fashion promises to be a positive and even intellectually exciting experience for the teachers involved. The more familiar the teachers become with the system, the easier it goes. I once conducted a demonstration scoring session with a college English faculty simply to acquaint them with the process. After about 45 minutes of scoring papers (just for practice), I suggested it might be time to wind it down. The group objected and insisted on at least another 30 minutes.

GENERIC AUTHORING SOFTWARE

The software that would best serve the development of such an information system would be generic authoring software as opposed to a hard-wired system. A generic authoring system would create the shell or system into which the school staff would enter information from his or her own subject field relative to content and performance standards. For each performance standard, rubrics and sample work products would be included. A hard-wired system with content standards and performance standards already built in, along with screens, aides, and prompts for the standardization of teacher judgments, would be tantamount to a national curriculum. One size would certainly not fit all in this case.

The actual software a school district ends up using would best be authored via the generic authoring system at the school, school district, or state level. A most feasible approach, as described later in the Epilogue, might be having the system developed collaboratively by a consortium of like-minded schools and school districts. The closer the system is developed to the end-users, the better it would be. Ownership by the users is essential.

It is conceivable but only remotely possible that the authoring system might come with a completed prototype or sample system already developed to serve as a point of departure. Some schools might prefer to tinker with an existing sample system rather than build their own.

Once completed and in use, the new software system would become an important part of the school's and school district's data warehouse and the centerpiece in the local accountability information system.

12

How an Instructional Management Information System Would Work

An instructional information management system makes possible the systematic querying of teachers drawing on their own observations and standardized judgments of student knowledge and skills. A procedure of this sort would provide the most direct, valid, and efficient source of information for instructional management and accountability. Let's envision such a system step by step.

GETTING STARTED WITH THE SYSTEM

For such a system to work, careful thinking and experience with the content standards and assessments must be incorporated into the system before the classroom teacher begins to use it. The software system itself would be an authoring system into which the school or school district could input its own academic content standards; benchmarks by grade level; performance standards at basic, proficient, and advanced levels, scoring rubrics; and sample student products. As the school or school district moves toward adopting such a system, a two-year planning/implementation period would be reasonable. This would allow time to fully develop the academic content and performance standards and incorporate them into the computer system.

As noted earlier, the system would require a computer on every teacher's desk, linking the teacher to the information system. (This computer may be a laptop that the teacher could use at school or, in a more limited way, at home.) Once the system was in full swing, the teachers would begin each year or semester by receiving group profiles of the students in each of their classes. After reviewing this readiness information, teachers would then select in the computer program the academic content and performance standards they would pursue with each class. From this, they would have their observation/assessment agenda laid out for them for each class. The instructional manager would also have a school-wide picture of the coverage of the academic and performance standards schoolwide in real time, which would provide a sufficient interval to address noteworthy gaps or inappropriate overlaps in the coverage. For example, a class might be slated to pursue a standard they had attained in a previous class, or perhaps the teachers are all assuming certain writing skills are being covered by other teachers.

Besides the content included in the school's content standards, teachers could continue to select content they wish to include in their teaching in each class. This additional content would be noted in the information system. While providing the core of the program, the academic content and performance standards would be designed to leave room for teacher-selected content. In their grading, teachers would be looking at student progress on the selected content and performance standards and on the additional content.

RATING AND REPORTING

During each quarter, every student would be rated in the system at least once or twice on the performance standards addressed that quarter. From these ratings, the teacher could call up from the system a group-profile of performance. When teachers begin to assign grades, they can see at once how these grades relate to their ratings of student mastery of the standards. If relevant test score information is available in the data warehouse, teachers could look at how proposed grades compared to test scores for their students in each class. Teachers would be among the primary users of this system.

At each grading period, parents and students would receive a report card with both the grade for the term and the students' individual ratings on each performance standard showing mastery at one of the following four levels, in progress, basic, proficient, and advanced. For the first several years with the system, these individual ratings would be labeled as "tentative," until the staff felt comfortable with these ratings for individuals. Group-average ratings would tend to be more trustworthy. Thus, the ratings, when used for group purposes such as accountability, would be useful from day one.

With explanations provided to parents on the performance standards, parents would themselves be in a position to verify (or specifically investigate) their child's rating in everyday skills like writing a simple or complex sentence or adding two-digit numbers. The information system would provide parents and students with important information both about what the teachers are teaching and what each student is and should be learning. These answers go to the heart of the accountability questions.

MANAGING THE SYSTEM

Using the system both teachers and instructional managers could see how attendance, deportment, extra-curricular activities, etc., relate to student mastery of the standards and to student grades. They could see these patterns in real time, with time enough to intervene. For example, students might be progressing successfully with most of the performance standards being covered at their grade level and then evidence great difficulty with one certain standard. Seeing this possible problem, the teachers and the instructional manager can confer immediately and devise a remedy on the spot.

Instructional managers would also be able to see in real time apparent barriers to student learning and begin to seek remedies. Instructional managers could, in addition, work with teachers to assure semester exams in part provide data that help to corroborate the standardized judgments the teachers entered into the system. The systematic and ongoing validation of the system would be a primary responsibility of the instructional managers. An important and entirely appropriate role for external, standardized testing is to be a source of information on the validity of the data generated by the information system. The public has become accustomed to trusting external, standardized tests precisely because they are standardized and external, i.e., not developed and scored within the school. Appropriate use of these tests might, however, require instructional managers to get inside the tests to identify those sets of questions that match their school's own content and performance standards. The total score in some standardized tests, though perhaps noteworthy in itself, may not address the question of the validity of the standardized judgments of teachers. Certainly, college admissions tests like the SAT I and the ACT do provide valuable information, but they might not be useful for validating any given school's information system, especially without question-by-question data, which are not available. State and district-wide assessments and commercially developed tests are most likely to serve as sources of validating information.

13

Providing a Truly "Public" Education via the Internet

While Internet access is not yet universal for every family having a computer at home, the majority of families with students do have Internet access. In addition, with access at public libraries, at work, at a friend's house, etc., the Internet is for practical purposes universally accessible to those who are interested. The Internet can make accessible to parents and the community the kinds of information that would satisfy demands for accountability by schools. The Internet can make schools, be they public or private, truly "public," by sharing information, whereby the public can readily know what and how well schools of all kinds are doing.

TELLING THE SCHOOL'S STORY USING THE INFORMATION SYSTEM

Taking advantage of the information system that capitalizes on teacher judgments that are standardized (i.e., backed by clear evidence), the school's web site could provide students, parents, and the community with the following information grade by grade:

- group reports showing the percent of students at the basic, proficient, and advanced levels on each of the academic content and performance standards. These reports will show what is being taught and what is being learned.
- group reports on the number and percent of "A" students, "B" students, etc. at each of the levels for each of the standards covered. This report will show what grades on average mean in performance terms and how they make sense in performance terms.

- group reports on the average scores on standardized tests for "A" students. "B" students, etc., where appropriate. Reports of this type will show how the school's standards make sense related to test scores.
- group reports showing attendance and conduct data related to the mastery of standards, which will show how much attendance and conduct are problems and how they affect learning.
- group reports relating mastery at the three levels and performance on relevant standardized tests. These reports will show how the school's mastery levels relate to other measures of performance and to the performance of national norm groups.

Reports with such a scope will give the best answers possible to the accountability questions most people ask. By looking at grades and the mastery of performance standards, the public can see what any individual school is doing and what kind of grading standards the school has.

With access to the Internet, people can quickly access the data that interests them without having to wade through what is not of interest to them. A school website on the Internet also spares the school the huge costs of printing and mailing reports to parents and the entire community, if the latter is even possible. The website would show grade by grade in each subject field the standards being covered and how well the students are mastering each standard. Such a website would fully inform the community on what is being taught and what is being learned, the fundamental questions behind the quest for accountability.

FEEDBACK VIA THE INTERNET

The Internet can do a lot more for schools besides effective reporting. Parent and community surveys on questions of the day can be easily conducted and instantly reported to the school staff and the community. My first direct involvement with the use of the Internet in polling a community involved a national survey funded by the McCormick Tribune Foundation to identify widely accepted content specifications for the test of U.S. History and Government, administered by the Immigration and Naturalization Service (INS) to people seeking to become American citizens. The survey revealed a broad consensus on what should and should not be included in the test. With the project's Internet expert, I naively suggested we needed to set a date for tallying and printing the survey results, the way we did in testing with answer-sheet processing. The expert then reminded me that scoring and reporting on the Internet were instantaneous, with printing requiring only a tap on the PRINT key.

School managers could offer on the school's website brief and timely surveys on current hot topics. Other surveys could address important basic questions, such as which skills are most valued by local employers likely to hire young people, as discussed in chapter 17. Such surveys would encourage people to view their schools as valuable sources of information.

The potential for online assessments has hardly been touched. Andrew Trotter in *Education Week* reported on pioneering efforts in Oregon and elsewhere to move their state assessments online.[1] The ETS online-testing expert, Randy Bennett,[2] saw these efforts as baby steps in a complicated evolution toward online testing which "is going to happen." Bennett adds, "It's very clear as kids become used to and routinely do writing on computers, paper and pencil tests don't do a fair job of determining their skills. . . . Tests that are delivered in a mode that's different from the one in which students are learning will eventually become indefensible. They won't be credible to parents, teachers, and students (and) . . . in the end . . . to the testing community." This suggests some challenging days ahead for state assessments and other external standardized tests.

Online testing offers immense advantages. Online testing provides instant scoring and reporting. It eliminates all the business of printing, shipping, distributing, collecting, returning sheets for scoring, and the printing and distribution of reports required for paper and pencil testing. This in turn allows for the "just in time" delivery of tests. Students can be tested after they complete the entire course and in time for their final grades. At present, students are tested in March, so that the results can be returned before the school year is completed, a schedule that leaves much material uncovered at the time of the test. Online testing also can provide for adaptive testing in which a student answering correctly (say) the first ten questions can be advanced to a more challenging level of questioning for the next ten.

The rich potential of online testing would be liberated from many security and other constraints by being integrated into an instructional management information system that features the standardized judgments of teachers. In this context, online testing would not be the special event testing for which students are hyped and primed. It would be an everyday kind of testing, which would add to the evidence the teachers could use in rating their students. These tests would be viewed chiefly as learning exercises that show results. There is no limit to the numbers and kinds of online tests or learning exercises that students would have a chance to complete.

Textbook publishers could be encouraged to offer online end of unit assessments that could be assigned as homework or done during class. For example, a geography teacher who had just completed a chapter on Mexico could ask the students to complete the assessment on Mexico in (say) the next two days. Instant scoring would benefit both the teachers and the students. The teacher could instantly access a roster of individual scores and group/class profile displaying the results of the test about Mexico.

The sheer number of tests in play would eliminate the traditional cheating strategies, which were designed for special-event tests. Students might complete one or two tests or learning exercises a week in each subject. With all the possible tests the student could be called upon to take, it would be easier to learn the subject than to cheat. Anyway, the validity of the results from one of these tests or learning exercises would always be decided by the teacher. A score from one of these tests or learning exercises would be just one piece of information teachers would have, as they make their judgments on what students can and cannot do.

Because many textbooks are used nationwide, computer scoreable tests or learning exercises would, in fact, work like standardized assessments; they would be scored online to give instant results as a service to teachers and students alike. These results would show how individuals or class groups compared to the large number or students also using this text and these assessments at the same grade level.

Publishers, however, would be encouraged to use a variety of question formats to get beyond factual recall questions. Each test or learning exercise would include, as a hoped for rule, questions that required application and thought.

Textbook adoptions are big business. Perhaps someday soon, one criterion used in textbook adoption would be the quality of a textbook publisher's online assessments. These same tests or learning exercises used nationwide or worldwide would give textbook publishers a valuable picture of how students are managing with the material they are offering. Successes and barriers in learning would be easily identified. These same data could be looked at district-wide with equal benefit.

With a full menu of online tests or learning exercises from textbook publishers, parents could also get a running view of how their child was progressing, something akin to a streaming video on their students learning.

As a whole, the concept of the instructional management information system introduces a new way to think about using computers and the Internet in education, moving well beyond the present supplementary and reference uses. This new way of thinking will lead schools to so much new and better information, people will soon say, "Enough already with this accountability business!"

NOTES

1. Andrew Trotter, "Testing Computerized Exams," *Education Week,* 23 May 2001.
2. Ibid.

14

Rubrics and Grades: Getting Around the Curve

A stock criticism of grades is that they are inflated at all levels, including college. Grades continue to trend upwards with more A's recorded every year, while other general measures of academic proficiency show no such trend. For example, a 1998 College Board report noted that since 1987, the percent of students reporting grades from A− to A+ increased from 28 to 37 percent, while their average SAT verbal scores dropped 13 points and their math scores dropped one point. ACT has reported similar trends.[1] College-bound seniors reported different average grades by subject fields with arts and music grades as the highest (3.7) and math grades as the lowest (3.0). Inflation is one of the difficulties with grades. Grade inflation is clearly not limited to elementary, middle, and high schools. In 2001, it came to light that Harvard awarded A's to 51 percent of its students and had 91 percent graduating with honors.[2]

ADDITIONAL PROBLEMS WITH GRADING

Grading is something of a mare's nest. There is a constant pressure toward inflation; everyone seems to feel better about good grades, however much or little they are deserved. What goes into grading varies from teacher to teacher. Greg Cizek described what he called the "kitchen sink" phenomenon. "Nearly everything is considered when assigning grades. . . . Teachers want to consider any relevant aspect of a student's classroom experience. . . . Unfortunately, no consensus exists—even within school buildings—about which factors are relevant."[3]

A number of researchers have found that, as a pattern, the more able students tended to be graded on their achievement and the less able students

75

on their achievement *plus* other factors, such as effort. In this context, Cizek cites the research on self-concept and achievement, which has shown a weak to non-existent relationship between the two or a relationship that works in the opposite direction. That is to say, students first show some achievement and then feel better about themselves.

The most pernicious doctrine concerning grading is the ancient, shamefully venerated doctrine of "the curve." This is the bizarre notion that the normal distribution curve is replicated in every class group, regardless of how well or how poorly the subject matter is taught. In many instances, teachers must search for nits in their students' work to distinguish between one point on the curve and the next. Grading becomes an essentially negative experience for both the teachers and the students in such cases.

Krumboltz and Yeh lay bare the evils of what they call competitive grading: "To assign grades, teachers must become critics whose focus is negative. Moreover, students must be compared with one another, because there is no accepted standard for a given letter grade. A performance that earns an A in one classroom could earn a C in another classroom because of differences in the teacher's standards or in the composition of the two classes."[4]

Some might argue that this kind of competitive grading is necessary because colleges and others depend on schools to carry out a sorting process. The answer from Krumboltz and Yeh is that's the colleges' problem. Let them work it out. A grading system tied to performance standards and focused on positive achievement, would end up, nonetheless, with some sorting but without any preconceptions about the normal curve. Differences of some kind are likely to remain.

STANDARDS AND RUBRICS

In the first chapter, we described an instructional management information system that would routinely display grades together with teachers' ratings of their students' level of attainment of content and performance standards. These displays are likely to have a salutary, clarifying effect on grading practices. Teachers, instructional leaders, parents, and students will want these to make sense. Students getting A's should be doing advanced work on the content and performance standards more often than students with B's, and so on. These displays will treat grades entirely as a measure of attainment, as opposed to a combination of attainment and effort or good-heartedness.

Rubrics and Grades: Getting Around the Curve

When a grading system includes a focus on rating students in refere academic content standards, the system must report on achievemen effort separately. Both are important. As will be noted in chapter 17, among the "skills" employers value most are those related to effort, such as attendance, punctuality, completion of the assigned work, etc.

A development of landmark importance in connection with content and performance standards is the introduction of what is called the "rubric." In traditional prayer books used by some churches, instructions printed in red tell the clergyman what ritual actions to perform as the prayer (printed in black) is said. These instructions in red came to be known as "rubrics."

In today's schools, where rubrics are being used, they are supposed to represent clear and concise descriptions of the kind of work associated with a point on a scale describing a certain level of performance. If a "5" is the top of the scale, the rubric for this score point would describe the features of a "5" paper. These features would be more impressive than the features described in the rubric for a "4" or "3" paper and so on. In a fully developed scoring guide, samples of work would often accompany and illustrate a set of rubrics.

EXAMPLES OF SCORING RUBRICS

The following examples of scoring rubrics are taken with slight modifications from the web site of CRESST, a national center for assessment research and services at UCLA.

The first rubric in Figure 14.1 is designed for use in assessing the mechanics of writing based on a sample of writing.

In each rubric score point, there is a summary description followed by a more detailed description of the work that characterizes the score point. Rubrics concentrate entirely on the quality of the work and not on how one student's work compares to another's. Rubrics are at the heart of standards-based schooling.

The second rubric in Figure 14.2 using a 5-point scale is designed for use with an essay response to a knowledge related question or topic.

Using rubrics with samples of work is the complete antithesis to a mindless grading on the curve. If "5" is the top score, clearly explained in the rubrics, and if all of the students earn an advanced rating by doing "5" level work across the board, then they all would get A's. The issue of grade inflation goes away at this point, when the grades and the rubric-based

Figure 14.1

Score Point	Criteria
4	**Proficient** **There are few or no minor errors. There are no major errors.** The student has it down. There are few careless mistakes. The answer is well written.
3	**Adequate** **There are some minor errors, a few major errors.** There are some obvious types of mechanical errors, but overall the student's writing is adequate.
2	**Readable** **There are numerous major and minor errors, but the meaning is still clear.** There are many errors, both serious and minor. The author's message is clear despite the fact that the answer is riddled with spelling, punctuation, sentence construction errors, etc. The writing is not adequate.
1	**Unreadable** **Errors are so numerous and serious that they interfere with communication and it is difficult to tell what the student is saying.** It is so poorly written that you cannot be sure what the student is trying to say. There are lots and lots of mistakes which make it hard to read and understand.
0	**The student left the answer blank.**

Figure 14.2

Score Point	Criteria for Scoring
5	***Complete Mastery Evident*** • The student is extremely knowledgeable about the topic. • The student demonstrates in-depth understanding of the relevant and important ideas. • The student includes the important ideas related to topic and shows a depth of understanding of important relationships. • The answer is fully developed and includes specific facts or examples. • The answer is organized somewhat around big ideas, major concepts/principles in the field. • The response is exemplary, detailed and clear.
4	***General Mastery Evident*** • The student has a good understanding of the topic. • The student includes some of the important ideas related to the topic. • The student shows a good understanding of the important relationships. • The answer demonstrates good development of ideas and includes adequate supporting facts or examples. • The answer may demonstrate some organization around big ideas, major concepts/principles in the field. • The response is good, has some detail, and is clear.
3	***Limited Mastery Evident*** • The student demonstrates some knowledge and understanding of the topic. The overall answer is OK but may show apparent gaps in his/her understanding and knowledge. • The student includes some of the important ideas related to the topic.

		• The student shows some but limited understanding of the relationships. • The answer demonstrates satisfactory development of ideas and includes some supporting facts or examples. • The response is satisfactory, containing some detail, but the answer may be vague or not well developed and may include misconceptions or some inaccurate information.
2	*Little Mastery Evident*	• The student has little knowledge or understanding of the topic. • The student may include an important idea, part of an idea, or a few facts but does not develop the ideas or deal with the relationships among the ideas. • The response contains misconceptions, inaccurate or irrelevant information. • The student may rely heavily on the group activity. • The response is poor and lacks clarity.
1	*No Mastery Evident*	• The student shows no knowledge or understanding of the topic. • The student writes about the topic using irrelevant or inaccurate information
0	**No Response**	The student either left the answer blank, wrote about a different topic, or wrote "I don't know."

performance ratings are displayed in the school's new online accountability system.

The rubric shown in Figure 14.3 is used to score each individual item on short-answer tasks. The goal for this rubric is to evaluate the degree to which a student has the knowledge and understanding needed to define a vocabulary term, or to answer a short question designed to elicit basic knowledge of a particular idea/concept.

Figure 14.3

0 – No Knowledge or Understanding
The response is characterized by **one or more** of the following: • No response. • A completely incorrect response. • Response conveys no understanding of a term as it relates to the test topic. • Response conveys no understanding of the idea or concept needed to answer the question.
1 – Minimal Knowledge and Understanding
The response shows that the student has some inkling of knowledge or understanding of the term. An example from the 5th grade Jamestown test: Native American: **Indian**
2 – Partial Knowledge and Understanding
The response is only partially and not complete. It might define the term but not relate it to U.S. History. The response is characterized by **one or more** of the following: • Partially correct answer. • Response conveys some but no complete understanding of a term as it relates to the test topic. • Response conveys some but not complete understanding of the idea or concept needed to answer the question.
3 – Full Knowledge and Understanding
The response is characterized by **one or more** of the following: • Completely correct answer. • Response conveys full understanding of a term as it relates to the test topic. • Response conveys full understanding of the concept needed to answer the question.

Figure 14.4

4 – Completely Effective Response

- The student selects and implements relevant concepts and procedures/strategies needed to solve this problem.
- The student considers all constraints of the problem situation.
- The solution and all relevant work are correct; or, there is a mistake due to some minor computational or copying error.

3 – Effective Response with a flaw:

The student selects appropriate procedures/strategies to solve this problem; however, the response/solution is not entirely correct because **one** of the following is apparent:

- There is evidence the student has **a** misconception or has failed to consider **a** relevant concept needed to solve the problem correctly.
- The student fails to consider **a** constraint of the problem situation.
- The student has considered **an** irrelevant variable or failed to consider a relevant variable.

The response/solution is generally correct; but only limited information is provided on how the student arrived at this solution.

2 – Response Incorrect with correct steps or Correct with no steps shown

The student selects appropriate procedures/strategies to solve this problem; however, the response/solution is not correct because **one or more** of the following are:

- There is evidence that the student has **several** misconceptions or has failed to consider **several** relevant concepts needed to solve the problem correctly.
- The student fails to consider **several** constraints of the problem situation.
- The student has also considered **several** irrelevant variables or failed to consider **several** relevant variables.
- The student did not carry the procedures/strategies far enough to reach a solution.

The response/solution is generally correct; however, there is no information showing how the student arrived at this response/solution.

1 – Response shows attempt only
An incomplete and/or incorrect response/solution is provided **evidencing an attempt** to solve the problem. In addition, one or more of the following are apparent: • The student did consider a constraint or variable of the problem situation. • The student understands some concepts relevant to the problem task. • The student selected a totally inappropriate procedure/strategy.
0 – No Response
• It is blank. • The student response only repeats information in the problem task. • An incorrect solution/response is given and no other information is shown. • The solution/response and supportive information is totally irrelevant to the problem task.

Figure 14.4 above presents a 4-point scale or rubric for evaluating the response to a problem-solving task. It takes into consideration the level of student knowledge and understanding with respect to the given problem solving task; the selection and implementation of appropriate procedures and/or strategies; and the accuracy of the solution obtained.

Scoring rubrics should not come as afterthoughts; they should be developed upfront, before the lesson is taught or the work is assigned. Students should be familiar with the rubric for a task as they undertake the task. Heidi Goodrich, an expert on rubrics, quotes a student who complained about the use of rubrics, "if you get something wrong, the teacher can prove you knew what you were supposed to do."[5] The rubric, for example, for an assigned essay tells both the teacher and the students the features of an essay rated as "advanced."

Goodrich explains why teachers should use rubrics:

• They help students and teachers define quality in concrete terms.
• Students using rubrics begin to accept more responsibility for the end product and stop asking, "Am I done yet?"

- Rubrics reduce the time spent in grading and explaining the grades and how the student can improve.
- Parents like the rubric idea; it helps them as they work with their children.

Rubrics and samples of work at each score point are essential elements in the scoring of open-ended work such as writing exercises and lab reports.

Rubrics are, in effect, observational rating scales that enable teachers to observe and record student attainment in a systematic and consistent manner. They are essential to the process of rating students in terms of their level of mastery on content and performance standards, as called for in the instructional management information system discussed here.

Rubrics cry out for incorporation in a computer-based instructional management information system. Only in such a system would they fully be utilized and likely to continue in use. In paper and pencil form, rubrics will prove to be too cumbersome to use, even superficially. In such a computer-based system, rubrics would enable teachers to carefully rate students' work in some detail with only a few clicks. With a few additional clicks, the teacher could aggregate this information into valuable individual and group instructional profiles, all in real time. An instructional management information system will require extensive use of rubrics, and any extensive use of rubrics will require such an information system.

NOTES

1. "High School Grading Policies," *Research Notes,* The College Board Office of Research and Development, RN-04, May 1998.
2. Harry Mansfield, "To B or Not to B," *The Wall Street Journal,* 20 December 2001, p. A16.
3. Greg Cizek, "There's No Such Thing as Grade Inflation," *Education Week,* 17 April 1996.
4. John D. Krumboltz and Christine J. Yeh, "Competitive Grading Sabotages Good Teaching," *Phi Delta Kappan* at www.pdkintl.org/kappan/krumbol.htm
5. "Just what is a rubric?" *Reforming Middle Schools & School Systems, Changing Schools in Long Beech,* (Vol. 1, No. 2 – Spring 1997) www.middleweb.com/CSLB2rubric.html

15

A New Credential: Certified Instructional Manager

The goal of the instructional management information system described in the preceding chapters is to have the local school be the primary source of accountability information. To do this, the school staff would use an instructional management information system that features "standardized" or publicly interpretable teacher judgments on their students' attainment of the school's content and performance standards. To attain this objective, there is a critical need for much more expertise, especially in assessment and technology, than is currently found among today's teachers and administrators. There is need to develop what could be seen as a new specialty area in educational administration called "Instructional Management." At a research meeting in 2000, R. J. Stiggins presented a paper[1] with a title that tells the whole story. The title was "Classroom assessment: A history of neglect, a future of immense potential." The challenge is how to move from a tradition of neglect to reach the potential, which is indeed immense.

For several months in 1996–1997, I had the opportunity to work as a consultant with senior staff from the three national associations of educational administrators, the American Association of School Administrators (AASA), the National Association of Secondary School Principals (NASSP), and the National Association of Elementary School Principals (NAESP). These three associations, which traditionally have worked independently of each other, were exploring ways to come together to sponsor a new, advanced certification for school administrators. While states already have licensing requirements for superintendents and principal, associations representing them wanted to go beyond that. Licensing is meant to assure the public that the people who are leading their schools have had at least the minimum preparation needed. Licensing is by its

85

nature *de minimis*. Licensing should never be a device for screening a pool of candidates, all of whom are presumed to be competent.

The certification being explored by these three associations was indeed advanced and beyond *de minimis*. The key to any such certification, new in education, is the willingness of schools and school districts to recognize such advanced certification with additional pay and preferences in hiring and promotions. Merit pay for teachers has not worked and the master-teacher credentialing program seems to be far too cumbersome. For administrators, especially principals, assistant principals, and department heads, there is no way they can differentiate themselves effectively on the basis of any demonstrated, advanced expertise. These three associations were on the right track, looking toward an advanced certificate.

NEEDED: AN ADVANCED CREDENTIAL FOR ADMINISTRATORS

Nonetheless, if schools are to assume leadership in accountability and to implement standards in any real sense, there is a clear need for a new, advanced credential for principals and other senior school-level staff. The new credential would need to be focused on instructional management in the information age as a specialty. It would certify advanced, hands-on expertise in three areas: curriculum, assessment, and technology. Schools seeking to implement standards-based teaching and assessment using an instructional management information system would likely be willing to seek out and pay a bonus for administrators with this kind of credentialed expertise. Administrators with such knowledge could give teachers onsite instruction and hands-on help in developing their own skills and expertise in classroom assessment, which, in turn, would assure the input of quality data into the school's own information system. It would avoid the threat of "garbage in and garbage out." The active presence of Certified Instructional Managers in schools would help assure quality data and the appropriate and effective use of information.

The creation and administration of such a credentialing program nationwide is made extremely manageable by the Internet. In my own involvement with Internet programs, I have come across excellent software by an Arlington generic authoring software firm, which any group could use to deliver both their training and assessment via the Internet. The tools are already there. One quality nationwide Internet offering would be more easily created than hundreds of college courses or workshops. The

Internet is also more accessible for the target audience, persons already working full time in schools.

GROUNDWORK ALREADY COMPLETED

For such a specialty certification, much groundwork has already been completed that identifies the need for this expertise and spells out just what is required. Collaborative national efforts involving the administrator organizations and organizations involved with assessment and technology have come together to define competency standards.

In 1997, "Competency Standards in Student Assessment for Educational Administrators"[2] were defined by the AASA, NASSP, and NAESP in collaboration with the National Council on Measurement in Education (NCME). These standards incorporated the earlier (1990) standards for teachers developed by the NCME in collaboration with the American Federation of Teachers (AFT) and the National Education Association (NEA). This latter set of competencies describe, as I see it, the kinds of hands-on expertise that the Certified Instructional Managers would help teachers in their schools to develop. The broad phrasing of the competencies would need to be fleshed out with more specifics. For example, one competency speaks of "developing assessment methods appropriate for instructional decisions." This would entail the development of rubrics, as discussed in chapter 14. Assessing in reference to performance standards needs also to be highlighted. Many technical advances to support assessment have occurred since 1990.

The next standard for administrators is especially important. It speaks of knowing the appropriate and useful mechanics of constructing various assessments. It calls upon administrators "to play a critical role in the proper development and use" of assessments involving rubrics and performance standards. Certified Instructional Managers and teachers together can develop and use the kind of instructional management information system that will deliver on the goals cited above.

In November 2001, a separate collaborative effort with the same organizations, plus a number of others, published consensus Technology Standards for School Administrators,[3] specifically for superintendents and principals. These standards cover the whole array of technology uses in schools, including instructional technology. Under the heading of "Productivity and Professional Practice," one standard calls upon administrators to "engage in sustained, job-related professional learning using technology resources." The online Certified Instructional Manager program called for above would be a timely application of this standard.

The statements of competencies and standards outlined above, while valuable in themselves, would have their value multiplied by being incorporated in an online Certified Instructional Manager program.

NOTES

1. R. J. Stiggins, "Classroom Assessment: A history of neglect, a future of immense potential," paper presented at the annual meeting of the American Educational Research Association.

2. "Competency Standards in Student Assessment for Educational Administrators," Buros Institute, 1997, www.unl.edu/buros/article4.html

3. "Technology Standards for School Administrators," TSSA Collaborative, 2001, North Central Regional Technology in Education Consortium, ncrtec@ncrel.org

16

By-Product I: New Information for College Admissions

In previous chapters, we have described an instructional management information system managed by school staff credentialed as Certified Instructional Managers. Group results from this system describing students' attainment of content and performance standards would be published on the Internet, which has the effect of making local schools the primary source of educational accountability. Information published about schools would be generated from data regarding students' mastering of any given school's own course of study, not on results from an external standardized test, for which they are prepped and primed via a cram curriculum.

This same information system, as a by-product, could generate a new statistic based on the school's own curriculum, which would enable college admissions staff to better predict success in college. This new statistic was developed by Cliff Adelman, a Senior Research Analyst at the U.S. Department of Education, from a national longitudinal study of students, ages 16 to 30 and their high school and college transcripts.[1]

THE HIGH SCHOOL AND BEYOND STUDY

Adel man's study looked at what contributes most to students attending 4-year colleges and completing their bachelor's degree. The predictive validity of the SAT and ACT is currently identified by colleges based on how well these tests predict success in the first year of college as represented by college grades. This is not unreasonable, given the easy access colleges have to such data. Mobility and the high college dropout rates make later data harder to find. Nonetheless, Adelman argues that "the

89

bottom line" number that people like college administrators, state legislators, parents, students, etc. are looking for is how many young people actually finish four years of college and get their degree. The goal is completion, not simply persistence for a time without a degree. The statistic Adelman has developed predicts college completion.

According to Adelman, "this study tells a story built from high school and college transcript records, test scores and surveys of a national cohort from the time they were in 10th grade in 1980 until roughly age 30 in 1993. The story gives them 11 years to enter higher education, attend 4-year college, and complete a bachelor's degree." Test scores, in this case, refer to a "modified-SAT" that is given to these students in the 12th grade.

This study reported a bachelor's degree completion rate of 63 percent for all students by age 30 who attended 4-year colleges. For those who earned at least 30 credits the rate exceeds 70 percent. For those in highly selective colleges, the rate exceeds 90 percent. Of 4-year college students assigned to remedial reading, 39 percent completed their bachelor degree.

The current trend in college student mobility indicates that over 60 percent of the student cohort attend more than one college. On average, it takes young people five full academic years to complete their bachelor's degree.

INTRODUCING THE ACADEMIC INTENSITY/QUALITY INDEX (AIQI)

What Adelman found in this national longitudinal study was "that the academic intensity and quality of one's high school curriculum (not test scores, and certainly not class rank or grade point average) counts most in preparation for bachelor's degree completion." Adelman has developed and tested in this study an index or indicator of academic intensity/quality of curriculum. Let's call it for now the Academic Intensity/Quality Index or AIQI. This index consists of 40 gradations that differentiate students based on the various combinations academic course work completed in high school. These gradations take into account the number of courses in English, mathematics, science/core laboratory science, history/social studies, foreign language, AP courses, and the absence of courses in remedial math or reading. This index is "criterion-referenced "and not a zero-sum norm like high school class rank, curve-based GPAs, and test-based percentile scores. On the AIQI, as Adelman points out, "everyone can reach the top rung of the ladder." This becomes possible, however, only with a certain equality of opportunity in terms of the courses offered by the high school.

For those who attended college at any time and who scored high or in the top 20 percent on each measure, the pattern was as follows:

Percent Completing Bachelor's Degrees

In Top 20% on	Percent completing
AIQI	72
Modified-SAT	67
Rank/GPA	64

It could be that socioeconomic status has the same or a greater impact on college completion as the AIQI. Not so! Adelman found that 80 percent of those in the top 20 percent on the AIQI who had attended a 4-year college completed their bachelor's. Of those with the same background in the top 20 percent on SES, 72 percent completed their degree. SES does have more impact as the student's AIQI drops. In the middle 20 percent on the AIQI, only 40 percent completed their degree compared to 56 percent in the middle of the SES distribution.

In comparison to the "New Basics," identified as a rigorous pre-college program in the wake of *A Nation at Risk,* a widely published 1983 study, the AIQI is more rigorous. It excludes remedial courses and requires two units in a core lab science.

USING THE AIQI

In his report, Adelman presents a decision table for assigning grades on the AIQI that could be readily incorporated into an instructional information system such as we have described in earlier chapters. Thus, the cost of providing this new information would be close to nil. Adelman uses a 100-point scale with each gradation counting 2.5. A student with a perfect 100 would have the following record:

- 3.75 or more Carnegie units of mathematics with no remedial math
- highest level of math at trigonometry or higher
- 3.75 or more Carnegie units of English with no remedial courses
- 2 or more units of core laboratory science or 2.5 units in science
- 2 or more units of foreign language

- 2 units of history or 1 unit of history and 1 other unit social studies
- more than 1 Advanced Placement score

On this scale, students taking remedial courses could not have an AIQI score above 72. The AIQI could be easily computed and reported on the student's transcript, of which it is a summary. The AIQI would also guide and focus the student's choices toward what is likely to make a difference in their college completion.

The AIQI also underscores the necessity for students to have access to the full range of courses needed for future success. In some cases, schools might need to turn to online courses or distance learning to complete their offerings.

AIQI IMPACT ON ADMISSIONS

Would the AIQI be the silver bullet that brings down the SAT and ACT? Not likely! The AIQI will not meet all of the needs of the highly selective colleges, which, for example, already show a 90 percent completion rate.

The AIQI would, however, add another summary statistic in the admissions process, one based on students' work on the school's own program. College admissions people are constantly in search of summary numbers to include in their selection formulae, numbers such as GPA's, test scores, and class rank. The AIQI would be an important new summary number. Adding this number, in turn, should take away much of the pressure on the vast majority students as they approach the SAT or ACT, which would be seen as much less "life-defining." The AIQI would represent a significant step beyond standardized testing, made possible by long needed advances in information technology in schools.

NOTE

1. Clifford Adelman, "Answers in the Tool Box: Academic Intensity, Attendance Patterns, and Bachelor's Degree Attainment" U.S. Department of Education, June 1999, www.ed.gov/pubs/Toolbox/Part1.html

17

By-Product II: Making Academics Count in the Workplace

A few years ago, counselors in a Virginia high school conducted a survey of their students. Students were asked to identify their chief concern. The students' greatest concern was finding a job, which surprised their counselors.

Approximately five million students are enrolled in the junior and senior classes in U.S. high schools. Some 47 percent of these students work at least 25 hours per week during the summer months. A recent survey of college freshmen showed that 46 percent identified saving from summer work as an income source for educational expenses. Twenty-one percent reported holding a part-time job on campus, and 24 percent reported having an off-campus part-time job. As the costs of college continue to increase, the importance of employment as one source of educational funding will only increase. As a sign of the times, college admissions literature has begun to praise the educational merits of working part-time.

The late Albert Shanker first brought national attention to the disconnect between high school and work. He described American youth as shrewd, if not skilled. They understood that no one really looked at what they did in school. A number of efforts were launched in the wake of Shanker's comments. The National Alliance of Business had a project called "Making Academics Count" in which they encouraged employers to ask for the transcript or some kind of school record. I worked on two such ventures. One at ETS was a pre-Internet program called WorkLink. The second was an Internet-based program idea with the National Association of Secondary Principals called SCRIBE. This latter effort soon proved to be beyond the NASSP's venture capital budget and their subsequently redefined mission.

I believe a splendid opportunity in American education exists for some national organization to step forward to launch a self-sustaining national program that would address the disconnect that Shanker pointed out. To give it a name, I will call this program *Skillfile*. Such a program would draw local businesses into an effective, unobtrusive partnership that would have a significant, positive impact within the schools. Such a program would become even more feasible with the kind of instructional management information system proposed in earlier chapters. One component of such a system would provide data for the *Skillfile* record.

Based on my earlier work with employers and schools, here is how I think a *Skillfile* service would work. A *Skillfile* service would:

- offer an Internet version of a school record tailored to employers' needs. By using this employer-friendly record in their hiring, employers would directly motivate students and improve schools by making academics count in the work place.
- report high school attendance, self-reported high school and college grades by subject fields in regular and advanced courses, GPA's and *Skillfile* online assessment results, along with work experience, specialized training, and self-reported computer skills. All records would be in an easy-to-read, standard format designed for employers.
- provide a voluntary program that identifies motivated young people. Individual students in their high school and college years would voluntarily share their *Skillfile* record with employers.

Here is how the system would work. Using the online *Skillfile* system,

- employers post open positions for full-time, part-time, and summer work and then quickly review the records of those who apply.
- employers can indicate in their postings the skill levels needed in each posted position.
- employers, using keywords, can also quickly search the database with or without a posting.
- young people can create their own record, enter it into the database, and then use it in replying to job postings online.
- individuals can also print an attractive copy of their *Skillfile* record for use away from the Internet.
- young people can review the expected job skills listed by employers as they plan their own skill growth.

Skillfile could leverage state and regional school-to-work efforts. Some states and localities are developing new kinds of school achievement certificates or employment portfolios for use at the job interview. These special features can be noted in the *Skillfile* record where employers can find them using keyword searches.

The following are key features of *Skillfile* as envisioned here:

#1: Regional Skills Banks Managed by a Regional Host Agency— The youth job market is a local or regional job market. This market must be served by local or regional programs rather than national programs. The key to the *Skillfile* program is the Regional Skills Bank, hosted and promoted by a regional host agency such as the major Chamber of Commerce or Community College in a region. When employers and colleges and young people go to their own Regional Skills Bank, they unobtrusively begin to use the national *Skillfile* network as the underlying system. This national network will enable young people and employers using their Regional Skills Bank to have access to other states and local areas, just as persons using a local bank can enjoy ATM services nationwide. Thus, students who go away to college can use *Skillfile* to search for a summer job at home and a school-year job near their college.

#2: Focus on Employer Defined Skills—Employers use the term "skills" more broadly than educators. In addition to reading, math, information processing skills, etc., employers also include as skills showing up every day and on time, completing assigned tasks, following directions, etc. *Skillfile* will provide an Internet based system for students to request ratings from their teachers on these latter skills and for teachers to provide these ratings for the students' record. These are the skills the employers consider as most important, even ahead of the traditional academic skills.

#3: Skill Assessments Linked to Job Requirements—Employer surveys and interviews have made it clear that employers are likely to use records if they have skill assessment results they can readily understand and use. *Skillfile* will offer a number of online, instantly scored assessments of work-related skills, as shown below on the sample record. A number of the skills would be rated by teachers. The school portion of the record would be generated by the school's instructional management information system described in earlier chapters. As employers post their open positions, they would check off the skills and levels of skills they are seeking in applicants.

#4: *Skillfile* Services at Bargain Rates for Employers and Young People— Online employment services, as a rule, charge employers substantial fees to post job openings. The youth job market is not, however, a niche that can sustain such fees. Employers need to be attracted to this job market by low costs and the quality of applicants they can find here. In *Skillfile,* employers can sign up, post jobs with their required skills, screen applications for posted jobs, or search the database, all free of charge. Only when employers have identified, from potentially hundreds of relevant individuals in the database, the few they wish to interview, would there be a modest (fee for each record downloaded. Names and addresses appear only when a record is downloaded. This makes the system easy to use and a terrific value for employers, while encouraging them to give qualified young people consideration in their hiring.

All online services to young people would be covered by a modest fee. Students would then be able to build and maintain their records online, apply for positions, and take the online national *Skillfile* assessments a number of times. A manual, available online, would guide the students through the process.

An important consideration is equity. *Skillfile* must serve and not handicap disadvantaged or at-risk youth. Disadvantaged students more than others tend to experience the disconnect between schooling and life and work. This program focuses on skills that young people can readily learn and apply. *Skillfile* would create a practical opportunity for community-based organizations like the Urban League to offer tutorial services enabling disadvantaged young people to develop skills they can record and use at once. Building their own *Skillfile* record would give young people a greater sense of purpose at school.

A SAMPLE *SKILLFILE* RECORD

In earlier field-testing of this concept, employers welcomed the kind of record proposed here. It was what they wanted to see. They did not find the traditional school transcript readable for their purposes. Figure 17.1 shows a sample of a *Skillfile* record for a fictional high school graduate in

Figure 17.1

Skillfile File number: 74397   Date: 8/10/00   Last updated: 6/12/00

Name   Paul LaRosa   Date of Birth: 7/18/83
Address   2418 Walnut St
City, State, Zip   Bedford, MD 20688   High School Grad/2000
Phone   301-867-4521
E-mail   plarosa@aol.com   Non Minority

Faculty/Staff Ratings of Work Related Skill

Skills	*Ratings*	*N of ratings*
Attendance	Excellent	4
Punctuality	Superior	5
Completing Assigned Work	Superior	4
Teamwork	Good	3
Oral Communication (English)	Superior	4
Written Communication (English)	Excellent	3

***Skillfile* Online Assessment Results**

	Level (1-7)	*Date*
Technical Reading	5	1/00
Reading Charts, Graphs, and Tables	5	1/00
Workplace Math	6	1/00
Computer Concepts	4	1/00

Work Experience

Position	*Company*	*Date*	*Hrs. per week*
Sales clerk	Barnes & Humble Books	6/99-8/99	40

Reference: Mildred Smith 301-445-3907
Skills used: Customer relations, cash management

Computer Software Use Experience

Software	*Level of Use/Expertise*
MS WORD	Full use of main features, text and tables
MS EXCEL	Full use of main features, spreadsheets and databases

Information from School or College Most Recently Attended

Grade Point Average By Year in High School/ College

	Year: 1	2	3	4
High School	3.4	3.3	3.5	3.4
Post Secondary	NA	NA	NA	NA

Grades in Courses in Major Subject Fields

Major Fields	Types of Courses	
	Regular	Advanced
English Lang./Lit.	B,A,B	A

Math	C,B,B	B
Physical Science	B,B	
Social Science	A.,A,B,A	B
Computer Technology	A,B	A,B
Arts/Humanities	A,A,B	A
Health/Personal Development	A,A,A	
Vocational/Technical	A	A

Job-Related Courses/Training

Name of Course	Date	Final Grade	Skills Acquired
Computer Applications	1-5/99	A	Advanced use of Word and Excel Use of Publisher

Honors/Awards/Recognition

Description	Source	Date
Editor of school paper	Faculty/staff selection	9/99
Letter in Soccer	Coaches	5/98 &5/99

the class of 2000. In the skill ratings, skills and rating-scale descriptors are explained for the teachers as they make their ratings online. This same information is available for employers as they interpret these ratings. Race, ethnic, and gender data are recorded but are not reported with any individual's record. These data are for use by employers who have selected a number of records for a job opening and want to check the make-up of their applicant pool.

The name, address, phone number, e-mail address, and all references are not included with the record until the employer has selected this record for use/downloading.

Based on numerous sessions with employers, this is the kind of record that they would welcome and use to overcome the disconnect between school and work. Schools, students, and employers would all benefit from generating such a record as a by-product of an instructional information management system.

18

A 21st Century Federal Initiative in Education

Both the Republicans and the Democrats have education at the top of their agendas. People are looking for the federal government to somehow improve K–12 education. Unfortunately, the ideas that have been advanced are disappointing and dated. They rely on a mid-20th testing technology and do nothing to bring the information age into schools and classrooms. They could have been advanced for the election in 1900, as well as for elections in the 21st century. Meanwhile, the means to improve education are right in front of us in the information age, in which bank and grocery clerks and car inspectors have far more information at their fingertips than do teachers and principals.

The federal government could dramatically impact education by advancing or introducing the information age in American schools. Some years ago, the information age stopped at the schoolhouse door. The information technology now used in teaching and instructional management is vintage 19th to mid-20th century. When computers came into classrooms, they went to the back of the room for the students to use on occasion. They did not go to the front of the room on the teachers' desks, linking teachers and principals into an information-age network.

A FEDERAL INITIATIVE ADVANCING THE INFORMATION AGE

The federal government with its immense resources, combined with a national sense of urgency, is now in a unique position to underwrite the development of a generic computer-based instructional information management system that will bring the information age into schools and classrooms. This would move principals and teachers ahead of bank and grocery clerks.

The multimillion dollar cost involved in creating such a system is too great for local systems to handle. They are stretched keeping their aging specialized systems running. Generic authoring software would support and strengthen all districts and schools without the federal government taking over any of them.

By underwriting the creation of such a system, the federal government would save important new developments that could disappear because of the effort they require. The investment in recent years in the drafting of K–12 content and performance standards has laid the groundwork for an instructional management information system based on standards. Content and performance standards have created a common language for describing learning. An instructional management information system would deal with observed knowledge or skill acquisition in reference to performance standards. Used in such a system, content performance standards would move from the shelf and into the classroom as the very focus of day-to-day instruction and assessment.

By creating this new information system, the federal government would tap the most neglected resource in education. Within the school, the best information on teaching and learning goes uncollected. It is the teachers who know which performance standards are addressed and how the students are doing. America's schools invest $90 billion a year in developing a knowledge base in the minds of teachers, a base that they never seriously tap. A well-designed, computer-based querying of teachers drawing on their observations of student knowledge and skills would offer the most direct, valid, and efficient source of educational information. Research, albeit limited, has documented the validity of well-structured teacher observations for these purposes. The hardware for collecting such data and information has long been available at feasible prices.

An instructional information management system would link every teacher and principal with his/her own computer to the school's instructional management information systems. Such a system would utilize all of a school's databases, e.g., scheduling, attendance, health, etc. This would make possible the following:

- Teachers could receive with their class roster information on the class as a group and on the individual students they are about to teach in term of student attainment of performance standards to date.

- Teachers could identify the performance standards they have chosen to address in each course or class and enter these into the system.
- Managers could monitor the system to assure effective coverage of important performance standards as the semester begins and address gaps at once.
- Teachers could periodically enter their performance ratings on these performance standards and grades for each of their students.
- Teachers could see online how their grades related to their ratings and to relevant standardized test results entered by the school, where such scores are available.
- Managers could monitor in real time student progress on performance standards and address instructional problems as they arise.
- Managers could monitor the validity of performance rating compared to in-school and external standardized assessments.
- Managers could send to the community and to parents state-of-the-art reports on what they want to know, namely, what is being taught and what is being learned. These reports could include explanations of grades in terms of the knowledge and skills of "A" students, "B" students, etc. Such information could be made available on the school's web site.
- Managers could also provide reports that integrate attendance, deportment, and student-life information with student performance.

Applications such as the foregoing illustrate what such an information system would make possible.

Along with the above applications, the system could also put at the teacher's fingertips an immense array of instructional resources, again keyed to content and performance standards. In every school, be it public, charter, private, or whatever, every teacher should have all the help possible to make sure American kids reach consensus performance standards. In addition, textbook publishers could put online instantly scorable instructional exercises/assessments, which teachers could assign their students to complete as "homework."

Such a federally supported system would produce the results the American people are looking for. Young people learn what they study. A system that focuses teachers, students, parents and communities on content and performance standards will produce results and, in this case, results that can be documented.

ADDITIONAL BENEFITS

Other benefits will also be reaped. The demand for accountability in education, which is a demand for information about learning outcomes, has created undue emphasis on external exams, be they state assessments or college admissions tests. This has happened largely because the schools themselves simply have been unable to report on what is being taught and learned. The result, in turn, has been the unhealthy spread of various cram curricula within schools and in often expensive, out-of-school programs. These cram programs for external exams have often intruded on the schools' own courses of study, on which the students are graded. This would stop. Using this instructional information system focused on performance standards, the schools would become the primary source of accountability information. External exams would serve a more appropriate role as a supplement and validity check for the information provided by the schools. Students could then better focus their attention on their school's own course of study. In treatment terms, this new information system would not eliminate external standardized testing; it would simply reduce the horrible swelling and the pain.

Another benefit deals with grades. The integration of schools' grading scales with measures related to performance standards would enable instructional managers using the information system to control the heretofore persistent problems with grade inflation. Any school could produce clearly understandable grading scales. Well-anchored grading scales will have two important effects. They will enable college admissions officers to assign more weight to grades in their admissions formulae. Grades have continually served as the single best predictor of ability to do college work. Newly clarified grading scales should prove even better as predictors. In addition, well-defined grading scales tied to performance standards could end the nightmarish attempts by states to create high school graduation exams with a single passing score. High school graduation could then remain a matter of passing a specified set of courses with a specified minimum average grade, without compromising anyone's interest in standards.

Another benefit pertains to instructional leadership or management. The instructional management information system would, for the first time, create the knowledge base needed for instructional management or leadership. There has been much dissatisfaction with principals and the training of administrators regarding instructional management or leadership.

No surprise! It is difficult to manage a school when one's chief source of information comes months later from some external assessment that never gets integrated to the classroom level. This new system would provide the basis for a virtually new field of instructional management. An important responsibility of instructional managers would be working with teachers as their roles are affected by the demands and opportunities created by the new system.

CONCLUSION: IT IS TIME

The time has come for the federal government to add to its successes in education with ERIC and NAEP by underwriting the development of a generic authoring system for a comprehensive instructional management information system serving every teacher and the technical assistance needed to put this system in place throughout the country.

This initiative has a feature that adds to its attractiveness. It is a politically bite-sized initiative that can be launched and completed, with careful planning, all within four years.

Epilogue

This epilogue is a fictional account from the perspective of ten years later of what may have happened after the publication of the ideas in this book. This fictional account takes an optimistic turn. It describes how these ideas came to be accepted and implemented. From this vantage point, the critical events stand out clearly.

First, there was a year or so of increasing discussion and probing of the idea of an information system that would tell more quickly and clearly how well schools were doing. Testing was certainly not the best answer. Testing could, at times, raise more questions than it could answer. For example, early in 2002, the 2001 test results from the complex and sophisticated Maryland School Performance Accountability Program were still not published, because educators were at a loss to explain certain unexpected drops in scores.[1] These kinds of experiences encouraged interest in new ideas for a more direct approach to describing learning in schools. Prior to this time, ideas of this type had seldom even been discussed. During this same time, educators and school boards became increasingly concerned that schools were more and more viewed as test prep and testing centers at the expense of the school's own curriculum.

THE CRITICAL INITIATIVE

The breakthrough came with an initiative taken by a major software company (let's call it the ES Company) that invited schools and school districts to join with them in a collaborative Information Systems Consortium for the development of two software programs, ES Teacher and ES School/District. To belong to this Information Systems Consortium, the participating schools and school districts agreed to:

- provide a networked computer of a certain capacity to each of their teachers
- work with a mutually developed set of content and performance standards with some tailoring as an option
- invest staff time and expertise in the drafting of observation scales and scoring rubrics related to performance standards
- accept an implementation plan for the use of the new information system (ES Teacher), which involved integrating grades with performance ratings and sample testing for monitoring/validating the system
- implement the companion ES School/District software program that provides for data-warehousing and the school or school district Internet site
- lease both software programs for a discounted annual fee for a set period of time.

This invitation from the ES Company was accepted by some 100 school districts, some 15 private school, two Catholic diocesan systems, and 10 charter schools. With these agreements in place, the ES Company, funded by its own venture capital, began the development of the two software programs.

Ironically, this collaborative venture resembled one of the major initiatives in the creation of nationwide standardized testing. In 1930, a kind of collaboration with schools and school districts was begun as the Cooperative Test Service at the American Council on Education.

CONGRESSIONAL ACTION

This new information system could have come into being as a creation of the Federal Government developed with Federal funds in cooperation with schools and school system through a network of advisory boards. The resulting software would be in the public domain. Building the kind of political support needed for such a Federal initiative, however, would likely take more than 10 years to develop. The actions described below are more modest and more easily attained.

A legislative initiative followed quickly after the Information Systems Consortium was formed. This initiative led to an accommodation in the federal reauthorization of ESEA called the "No Child Left Behind Act" of 2001 that required every pupil from grades three to eight be tested in reading and mathematics. Schools and school districts could be exempted from such statewide testing if they had in place an instruction management information system that provided information on every student's mastery of content and performance standards in language arts and math from grades one to eight. Such an information system would also need to be validated periodically by the testing of a sample of students. The legal accommodation at the Federal level reflected the view in Congress that what was needed was solid information, not necessarily more testing. Legislators saw the information-system approach as contributing more to school improvement than the addition of external standardized testing.

Congress showed further support for the information-system approach by allowing many of the costs of consortium participation to be covered by Title I and a special federal grants program.

AN EXPANDED CONSORTIUM

Two to three years after the first invitation to schools and school districts, a second invitation was offered for membership in an expanded consortium with fewer demands for developmental work by the participating schools and districts. Some 2,000 schools and school districts accepted this invitation. They were encouraged by the positive results shown by the first participants and by the supportive federal legislation.

During this period, the ES Company partnered with a major not-for-profit testing company to implement the school to work *Skillfile* component, which was included in ES School/District Internet software. The testing company, in turn, began to work with Chambers of Commerce and other employer organizations to encourage employers to use the *Skillfile* service, which creates added incentives for students to develop their skills.

The expanded consortium began collaborating with the three national organizations of school leaders to develop an online training and certification program for those involved in instructional management and staff development, using the new information and Internet system. As a condition for membership in the consortium, schools and school districts would agree to create financial incentives for those qualifying as Certified Instructional Managers via this online program.

WIDESPREAD USE OF INFORMATION SYSTEMS

With the work of the two consortia completed, schools and school systems began acquiring the now widely marketed software without any consortium participation required. Within five years, most schools and schools systems were using some form of an instructional management information system for both better instructional management and accountability. School staff began focusing entirely on their own program. This focus and the increased clarity of purpose created by the use of rubrics and better data apparently contributed to significant improvements in the achievement of students at all levels. High school diplomas were backed up by an achievement profile for each graduate akin to the record used in the *Skillfile* service.

With these developments, external standardized testing did not disappear. It moved from a starring role to a supporting role, a monitoring and validating role, for which it proves especially suitable. In this sense, American schools moved "beyond standardized testing" and into the information age.

A DARKER VISION

In contrast to the above scenario, a different fictional take on the next ten years might amount to a simple projection of the present into the future. These ten years would see the value of the school's own curriculum being gradually diminished as the importance of external testing becomes more established. Teaching in schools will be "peak-oriented," with intense periods of focus on the anticipated contents of the external tests. Schools will be looked upon as test-prep centers and adopt the mores of the test-prep industry. The goals in schools will be focused on a generic competence rather than varied forms of excellence. The percent of students showing mastery will be the controlling statistic. Through all of this, the split world of schooling will continue where the teachers, students, and parents in one hemisphere will be chiefly concerned about grades. In the other hemisphere, the administrators, public officials, and the community at large will be concerned about school scores on external tests. Some college-bound students and their parents will be forced to work in both hemispheres, given the exaggerated role of college admissions tests. All of this adds up to the depressing vision mentioned in the Preface.

NOTE

1. Nurith C. Aizenman, "Testing Errors Didn't Cause MSPAP Swings, Panel Says" *Washington Post,* 24 Jan. 2002: B1.

Index

Academic analysis 44
Academic Intensity/Quality Index 90–92
Accountability 1, 2, 3, 4, 63
Achievement tests 35–36
ACT 7, 22, 36, 89
Adelman, Cliff 89–92
Advanced Placement Tests 14, 21, 38, 58–59
American Association of School Administrators 85
American School Board Journal 31
Apgar scales 19
Aptitude tests 36
Atkinson, Richard 38

BARZUN, JACQUES 16
Bench-marking 45, 48
Bennett, Randy 71
Bennett, William 42
Broward County Public Schools 44
Bushweller, Kevin 31

California Academic Performance Index 3, 8
Certification 86
Certified Instructional Managers 86–89
Chambers of Commerce 95

Cheating on tests 30–31
Cizek, Greg 75
Cleveland Public Schools, 57–59
Coaching schools 37
College Board 35–38, 75
Content standards 47–54, 61, 63, 100
Council for Basic Education 47–48
Cram curriculum 29–32, 61, 102
CRESST 77
Criterion referenced tests 21
Cross, Christopher 48
Cultural bias 15
Curriculum 25–28, 47
Curriculum alignment 27–28

Data averse 43
Data warehousing 44–45, 61–62
Doherty, Kathy 8
Doyle, Denis 44

Education Week, 8, 71
Elementary and Secondary Education Act (ESEA) 7, 107
ERIC 58, 103
ETS 4, 7, 17, 27, 42, 71, 93
External testing 1, 13–18, 102

Face validity 58
Factual recall 14

Index

Federal Government 99–103
Feedback via the Internet 70–71
Federal Government 99–103, 106–107
Florida Comprehensive Assessment Test (FCAT) 9
Finn, Chester 53

GAGNE, ROBERT 25
Gallup poll 17
Gellman, Estelle 36
Generic authoring software, 64, 100
Goodrich, Heidi 83
Gore, Al 42
Grade curve 76
Grade inflation 75
Grades 4, 42, 75–76
GRE Analytical Reasoning Test 27

Hill, Paul 54
Horace's compromise 26
Hoven, John 30

Inauthentic character 14
IBM Reinventing Education Grant 44
Immigration and Naturalization Service citizenship test 70
Information System Consortium 105–107
Information systems 26, 59–60
Instructional management 41, 85–88
Instructional managers 66–67, 85–88
Instructional management information system 41, 61, 65–68, 84, 100–101
Internet reporting 69–70

Kaplan, Stanley 7, 32, 37
Kentucky Instructional Results Information System (KIRIS) 31
Knight Higher Education Collaborative 43
Krumboltz, John 76

Linn, Robert, 8–9
Lake Wobegone phenomenon 20
Learning Landscape 44
Licensing 85–86

Maginot Line 2
McCormick Tribune Foundation 70
Maryland School Performance Accountability Program 105
Matthews, Jay 42
Meritocracy 14
Minority students 15, 43
MS Company 105–107

Nader, Ralph 17
National Alliance of Business (Making Academics Count) 93
National Assessment of Educational Progress (NAEP) 11, 103
National Association of Elementary School Principals 85
National Association of Secondary School Principals 85, 93
National Center for Educational Outcomes 2
New Jersey Core Curriculum Content Standards 48–53
Norm referenced tests 20
North Carolina 9
North Central Association of Schools and Colleges 2

Observational rating system 54, 84

Passport Portfolio Program 22–23
Performance assessment 14, 16
Performance levels 11
Performance standards 4, 47–54, 61, 63, 100
Pimental, Susan 44
Portfolio assessment 8, 18, 20, 22–23
Powers, Donald 37

Princeton Review 7, 32, 37
Public Interest Research Groups (PIRGS) 17
Public school choice 10

Raising the Standard, 44
Recognition knowledge 16
Regional accreditation 1–2
Reliability 20
Report cards 57
Robinson, Peter 57–60
Rock, Donald 37

SAT 7, 17, 29, 35–39, 89
Scholastic Aptitude Test 35–39
Scoring rubrics 58, 77–84
SCRIBE, 93
Self-study 2
Shanker, Albert 93
Shepard, Lorrie 30
Sizer, Theodore 26
Skillfile 94–98, 107–108
Skills as defined by employers 95
Special event testing 1, 7, 14
Standards-based education 47
Standardization 19–24
Standardized testing 1, 8, 13–18
Standardized rating scales 4–5
Standardized teacher judgments 58–60, 63

State assessments 7–12
State of State Standards 48
Stiggins, R. J. 85
Streifer, Philip

Teacher judgment 57–59
Tennessee Value-Added Assessment System 9
Textbook publishers 72
Test-based reform 26–28
Test specifications 27
Thomas Fordham Foundation 48
Training papers 63
Transaction processing system 60
Trotter, Andrew 71
Truth in Testing legislation 17

Urban League 96

Vander Ark, Tom 54
Validity 20

Wagner, Tony 54
Wisconsin researchers 10
Work sample 22, 58
Writing samples 8

Yeh, Christine 76

About the Author

The day after George Elford defended his doctoral dissertation at Indiana University, he was on a plane to Boston to meet George Madaus at Boston College. At the time, Elford was working with Catholic Education in the Archdiocese of Indianapolis and had initiated a large Midwestern study of Catholic education, which Boston College agreed to conduct. Initiatives have been a hallmark of Elford's career. Later, he moved to the National Catholic Educational Association where he, as director of research, initiated several studies to clarify and articulate the "philosophy" of Catholic schools. He was lured away from this post by an offer from George Madaus to work in Dublin on a study that introduced standardized testing in Ireland in a study to identify the effects of standardized testing.

Upon his return from Dublin, he began his twenty-year career with the Educational Testing Service, where he worked first with the elementary and secondary schools division. In his 1974 interview for this position, he discussed with several senior staff the idea of an educational information system, for which he suggested that the time had not yet come. He later directed the teacher programs division at ETS and then joined the Field Services division, serving as director of ETS Field Offices, first in Boston, then in Evanston, and finally in Washington, D.C.

While in the Washington office of ETS, Elford pioneered the movement of testing programs from the mainframe to the microcomputer with the advent of the desktop scanner. He also worked with the Immigration and Naturalization Service to create the first national citizenship testing program that community agencies viewed as fair, in contrast to the uneven oral examines conducted at the INS interview. He also developed the idea of a school-to-work record that would make academics count in the workplace.

The ideas developed in this present work can be traced back to a number of Field Services projects in what was then called "curriculum monitoring." The advent of the microcomputer and the Internet has transformed these ideas into the quest for an instructional management information system, for which the time has surely come.